Photographing the Fallen

Photographing the Fallen

A War Graves Photographer on the Western Front 1915–1919

Jeremy Gordon-Smith

Pen & Sword
MILITARY

First published in Great Britain in 2017 and reprinted in 2021 by
Pen & Sword Military
An imprint of
Pen & Sword Books Ltd
Yorkshire – Philadelphia

ISBN 978 1 47389 365 8

A CIP catalogue record for this book is available from the British Library.

Typeset in Ehrhardt by Mac Style

Printed and bound in India by Replika Press Pvt. Ltd.

Pen & Sword Books Limited incorporates the imprints of Atlas, Archaeology, Aviation, Discovery, Family History, Fiction, History, Maritime, Military, Military Classics, Politics, Select, Transport, True Crime, Air World, Frontline Publishing, Leo Cooper, Remember When, Seaforth Publishing, The Praetorian Press, Wharncliffe Local History, Wharncliffe Transport, Wharncliffe True Crime and White Owl.

For a complete list of Pen & Sword titles please contact

PEN & SWORD BOOKS LIMITED
47 Church Street, Barnsley, South Yorkshire, S70 2AS, England
E-mail: enquiries@pen-and-sword.co.uk
Website: www.pen-and-sword.co.uk

Or
PEN AND SWORD BOOKS
1950 Lawrence Rd, Havertown, PA 19083, USA
E-mail: Uspen-and-sword@casematepublishers.com
Website: www.penandswordbooks.com

Contents

Vlamertinghe Military Cemetery.

Acknowledgements

I am indebted to a number of people who have helped in one way or another as this book has come together: my wife Rosie who has remained patient and supportive throughout, even following me with our young son Joseph into trenches and war cemeteries in France; my father, Bruce Gordon-Smith who has helped foster my interest in history and keenly shared family archives with me; David Bawtree who relinquished a large swathe of material into my care which has allowed a small project to progress into this book; Donald Bawtree who provided me with scans of Ivan's 1919 diary; Geoff Spender at the Imperial War Museum Photographic Archive whose team has looked after Ivan's glass plate negatives, digitized them, and supplied a great many high-resolution images to me; Andrew Fetherstone at the Commonwealth War Graves Commission who has helped me with sourcing their archives; Alastair Baird who I met in Talbot House while on a photographic trip to the Ypres Salient (he drove me to all the locations I needed to find and regaled me with encyclopaedic knowledge as well as enthusiasm for my project); Liz Thomas who has allowed me to quote from her great-uncle Ted Bate's war diary; Anne Bryan who has allowed me to quote from her father-in-law Reginald Bryan's First World War memoirs; Clifford Jones, archivist for Christ's Hospital School, who provided useful information about Edgar Bawtree and a photograph.

I want to thank the staff at Pen and Sword, in particular Roni Wilkinson and Matt Jones, for enabling the publication of this book to a standard beyond my expectations, and allowing it to be profusely illustrated in full colour. Jon Wilkinson has designed an excellent jacket.

I would also like to thank a number of people who have looked through drafts of the book and have been a source of encouragement: my brother Richard, Edwin Pillans, Toby Campbell-Colquhoun, Karl Cavanagh and Alison Quinlan. I'm indebted to Alison for her help with proofreading.

Prologue

The theme of remembrance has become embedded in the British psyche and at the time of writing we are commemorating the centenary of the First World War. This has generated renewed interest and many, like myself, are exploring their own family involvement in the war, scouring attics and websites for memorabilia and information. Ever since I was a young boy I've enjoyed exploring history and developed a fascination with the two world wars. Naturally I became very interested in delving into family archives that related to those tumultuous times. I would learn about my family history through various artefacts that my father would show me from time to time. I grew up hearing stories of the Bawtree family at Clapham Lodge in Sutton, and in particular about Uncle Ivan and Aunt Viola who were both younger siblings of my great-grandfather Alfred Edwin Bawtree. Ivan was evidently good at recording and remembering a great many details about his life and family history. Today a wealth of material survives which I have been compiling over the years, culminating in this book.

The material was originally gathered from Clapham Lodge, where Ivan lived until his death in 1979, by relatives such as my father and David Bawtree (both great-nephews of Ivan). Many items had been passed to David by Ivan personally. David tells me that one day in 1974 he was visiting Ivan at Clapham Lodge and decided to show his two children the cellar where he had taken refuge a number of times during the blitz of 1940–41. While down there he discovered some cardboard boxes containing numerous glass plate negatives, evidently dating from the First World War. Ivan was unsure about what to do with these photographs from his war service and was contemplating throwing the lot out. David fortunately offered to contact the Imperial War Museum (IWM) to see if they would like to receive the collection. The IWM was only too pleased to receive what is now 'the Bawtree Collection': some 600 photos printed from the glass plate negatives and displayed in three very thick albums. There are also a number of original prints in other albums and envelopes. In 2013 the collection was largely digitized and can be viewed on the IWM website. Ivan told David that he used to make two copies of each photo: one for the Graves Registration Commission and one for himself. Anyone contacting the IWM Photographic Archive in respect of war graves from the First World War is directed straight away to the Bawtree Collection, the most extensive collection currently available.

When my grandmother died in 1991 my father inherited another swathe of family memorabilia, some of which came from Clapham Lodge. There was an old tuck box filled with all manner of interesting items such as albums of old photos of the Bawtree family and other relatives, and very old diaries and notebooks. I remember looking through it as if it was a treasure chest. There were plenty of items that appealed to my curiosity, most notably Viola's 'Episodes in the Great War' diaries which provide a lot of insight into life on the home front such as rationing and the Zeppelin raids. Another diary that caught my eye was that of my great-great-grandmother Matilda Bawtree from 1873, the year she got married, written with calligraphic finesse, although barely decipherable.

There was also an old writing desk that my grandmother had acquired from Clapham Lodge in which my father discovered two diaries from the First World War that belonged to Ivan. My grandmother was apparently oblivious to their existence. For me, this was the real treasure.

In the early 1990s my father took me to see Ivan's photographic collection at the IWM archives, having given me his 1917 and 1918 diaries. This was of great interest to me, especially as I was studying the First World War at school which had included a trip to the battlefields, memorials and cemeteries around Ypres and the Somme. I took the diaries to school, keeping them in a brass Princess Mary tin from Christmas 1914 that my father had bought me, and impressed my history teacher enough to warrant a mini-exhibition that was displayed just outside the classroom. I also transcribed the diaries and my father sent a copy to the IWM.

Ivan used 'The Soldier's Own Diary', published by Charles Letts & Co., to record his doings in 1917, 1918 and 1919. These diaries contain 'Useful Information Invaluable to every Soldier at Home or at the Front', such as bugle calls, flags, useful knots, glossary of military terms, and navigation by sun or stars. This is the 1918 diary.

Some twenty years later David Bawtree found some boxes in his loft that hadn't seen the light of day for many years. In them were Ivan's 1915 diary, numerous letters home, his brief memoirs, various prints and other items pertaining to his service as a war graves photographer on the Western Front. David passed the documents over to my father and this gave my dormant project a new lease of life. I now have an unusually large amount of archives on which to draw in my desire to create a literary and visually stimulating account of Ivan's war service,

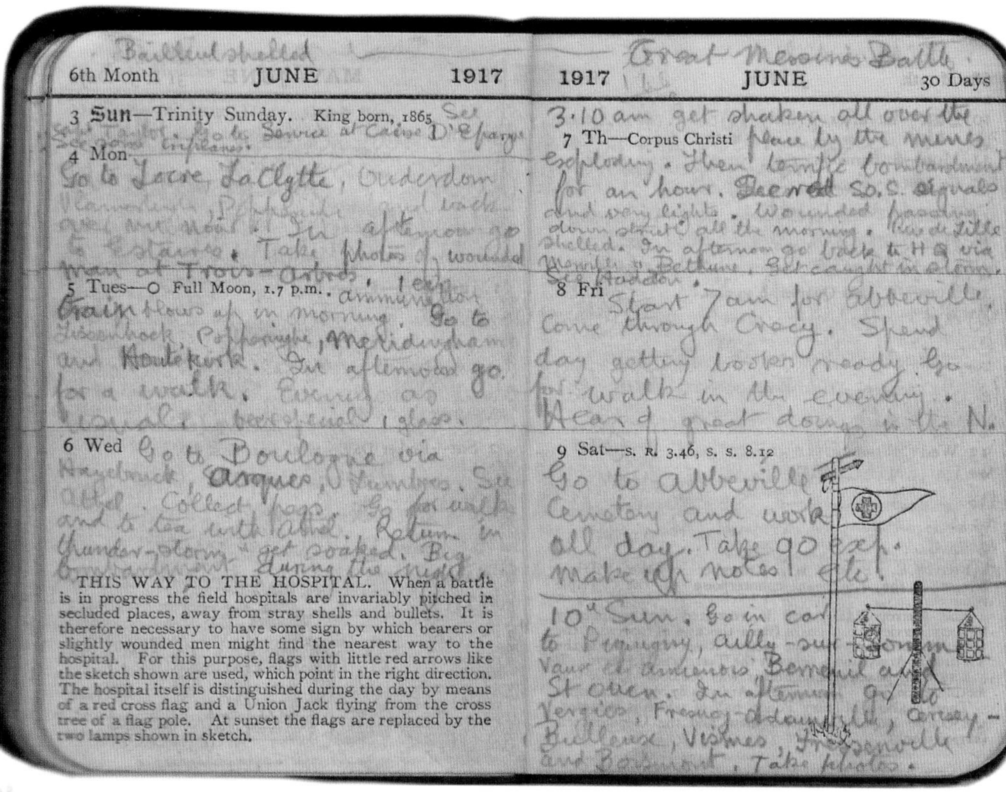

Ivan's diary from June 1917.

Ivan's family spent many a summer holiday in Charmouth. This photo, taken in 1910 by his sister Viola, is captioned: 'Each of the Coastguard Cottages had a large rainwater tank. Of these two in the picture one was no longer in use, being full of holes. My schoolboy brother, being keen on photography, converted it into his 'dark room' by pasting paper over the holes, and here he is shown, with dark lantern, about to disappear through the circular opening, over which he will slide the lid when he wants complete darkness.'

The oldest surviving photograph taken by Ivan was entitled 'A Moonlight Night (plate exposed all night long on Nov 7th 1911)'. It appears to have been taken looking out from his bedroom window.

and indeed the work of the Graves Registration Units that birthed the Imperial (later Commonwealth) War Graves Commission.

Photography has run in the family since its advent, the oldest surviving photograph being of Mary Ann Westfield, Ivan's maternal grandmother, taken around 1840. Many family photographs survive from the Victorian era, including some of the first years of Ivan's life. It is likely he took a keen interest in photography from a young age since both of his older brothers were proficient photographers, and by age 16 he was already experimenting and displaying technical knowhow.

After the war his brother Athelstan (known as Athel), who was an Associate of the Royal Photographic Society, started a developing and printing business from their older brother Alfred's attic and was subsequently able to build up sufficient business to open a shop on Station Approach, Sutton. The shop was called Camera Corner. Their sister Elaine worked in the office doing the accounts. Business would later shift from professional photography and printing to the sale of photographic equipment. Apparently the shop had a rather amusing sign in the window that said: 'God helps those who help themselves, but God help anyone who helps themselves here.'

Alfred was an electrochemical engineer and inventor who had worked with banknote engraving firms. He was a skilled photographer and won the astonishing accolade of being the first man to produce a record of sound on film that could be played back, long before the invention of talking film. He exhibited this discovery at the Royal

Photographic Society's exhibition of 1911. Subsequently he was made a fellow of the Royal Photographic Society for this work and his work on banknote security.

My father was frequently taking photographs throughout my childhood and beyond and always made sure I was suitably equipped for any school trip or holiday. I too have become a keen photographer and as such have included many of my own images in this book as I have sought to follow in Ivan's footsteps. I've visited many of the cemeteries and memorials in northern France and around the Ypres Salient in Belgium: row upon row of headstones, provoking sombre reflection. How would it have felt to have wandered among the vast numbers of wooden crosses of recently-dug graves of young men, captured through Ivan's lens? The level of loss suffered by countless households across the nation, throughout Europe and beyond, is unfathomable. Unlike British military campaigns today, this was a conflict on an industrial scale that enveloped the nation and directly affected everyone.

I would love to have been able to chat with Ivan about his First World War experience, something that others old enough in my family failed to do, or so it seems. It was common for veterans not to talk about the war or even refuse to do so, but in Ivan's case I sense from his many writings that he would have been amenable to such a discussion. He even recorded some audio memoirs in 1978 in which he briefly mentions the First World War. In some ways I feel as if I am completing a biography that he set in motion.

Ivan described his war experience as 'at times quite exciting', but also 'a gruesome kind of business.' A man of reserved character, he expresses little emotion about the grim and harrowing scenes that he mentions. He gives detailed accounts of where he went, what he did and what he saw, but feelings are understated. My father described Ivan as 'very practical and able to take things in his stride.' His writing often comes across as quite upbeat given the circumstances and there's a sense that he made the best of his time in France and Flanders. In respect of shellfire landing right near him: 'It was not always funny', or 'It made us think that did.' He, like most of his generation, just got on with it.

One of Ivan's colleagues, Corporal Reginald Bryan, described the work of the Graves Registration Units thus:

> It was really melancholy work and a rather sad task, but it was a necessary one, as apart from its sentimental value, it was necessary from a sanitary point of view. However, we didn't go about with long faces but tried to keep as cheerful and jolly as we could.

The text in this book largely draws on Ivan's own writings but does include material from several other sources, such as his sister Viola who was a fervent diarist, and

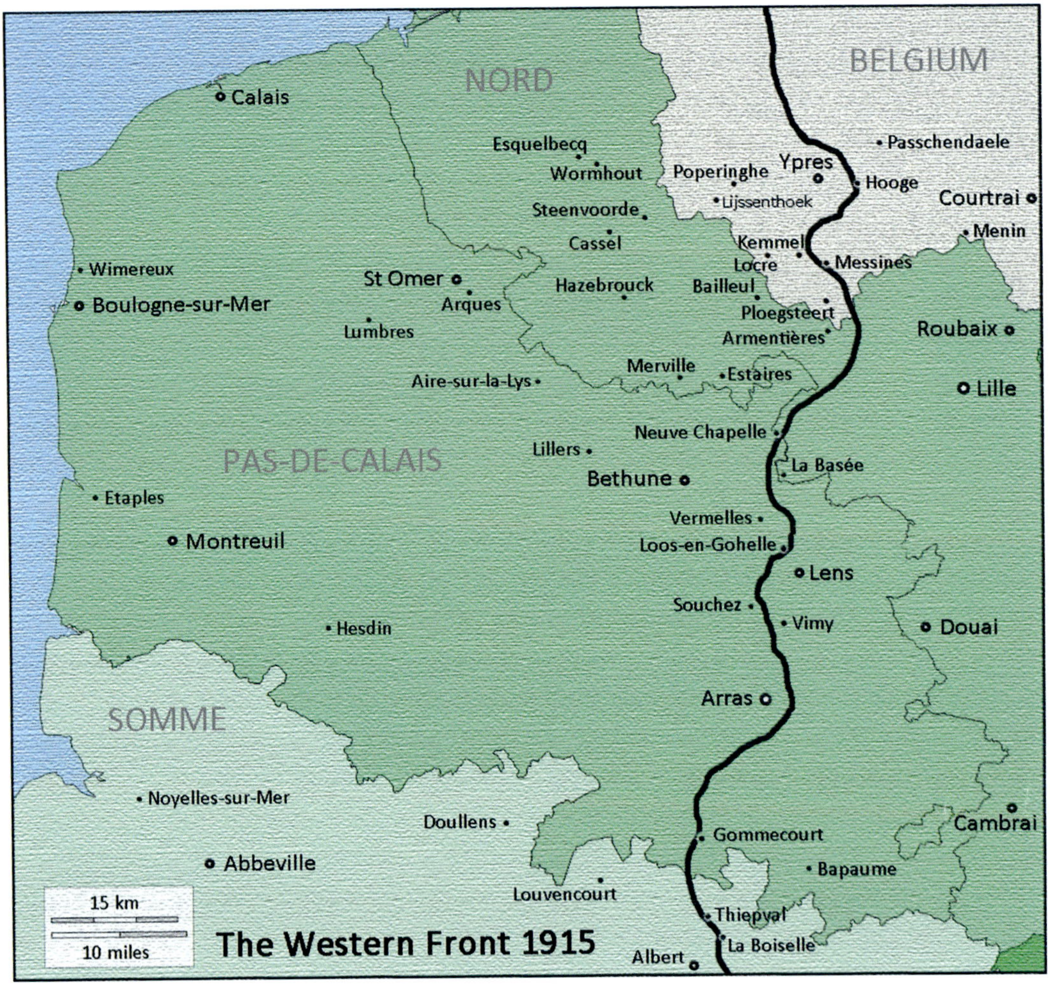

Map of north-east France and west Belgium showing the key areas in which Ivan moved around the Western Front and the front line as it was from June 1915.

archives from the Commonwealth War Graves Commission. All the black and white or sepia photographs are from Ivan's collection unless otherwise stated; all colour photographs have been taken by me in 2013–16. The glass plate negatives are all in black and white but since Ivan always toned his prints sepia, I have done this digitally. Some of the images have significant creases, rips or other blemishes which I have digitally removed or cropped out of the frame. In some cases I've been able to blend Ivan's photographs with mine, showing how wooden crosses have become headstones, shell-damaged cemeteries have become beautiful spaces of serenity, and how ruined buildings have been restored. While I have tried to keep the book as chronological as possible, I felt it necessary to draw on different themes, such as the dangers of the work, since that helps to draw the best out of the extensive material available.

Glossary of Abbreviations

AG	Adjutant General
AIF	Australian Imperial Force
BLB	Boys' Life Brigade
BRCS	British Red Cross Society
CCS	Casualty Clearing Station
CO	Commanding Officer
DAD	Deputy Assistant Director (of Graves Registration and Enquiries)
DGR&E	Directorate of Graves Registration and Enquiries
EFC	Expeditionary Force Canteen
GRC	Graves Registration Commission
GRU	Graves Registration Unit
IWGC	Imperial War Graves Commission
MC	Motorcycle
MG	Major General/machine gun
Mty Cty	Military Cemetery
OC	Officer Commanding
O i/c	Officer in charge
OR	Other Ranks
Pop	Poperinghe
RAMC	Royal Army Medical Corps
RE	Royal Engineers
TMB	Trench Mortar Battery
VAD	Voluntary Aid Detachment

Ivan in uniform attached to the British Red Cross, 1915.

Chapter One

Journey to the Western Front

Early Life

Ivan Lancelot Bawtree was born at Blackwater House, Sutton, Surrey on 12 January 1894 to Alfred Bawtree and Matilda Hephzibah Clark. He was the youngest of three brothers and three sisters. His parents were both from well-to-do families and employed a nanny, Nurse Thomas, with whom Ivan developed a close bond. The family was deeply involved in Sutton Congregational Church where his father was a deacon and his mother ran a women's Bible study group.

He described their home as 'a big old house with a large garden, formerly the property of a blacksmith whose forge was attached to the house. It was situated in the lower part of Sutton on clay soil and rather damp. Not a very healthy spot and not a good neighbourhood.' Apparently Ivan 'distinguished himself sometimes by wandering off and getting lost. Once they even searched the water duct for him.'

One of his earliest memories dates from 1897, when

> At the age of three, taken by Father and family for a picnic to Leith Hill, by train I expect. It was Queen Victoria's Jubilee celebrations and there was a huge bonfire built near Leith Hill Tower, nearly as tall as the tower. It was covered with a tarpaulin but when the time came to light it a man climbed to the top and I remember being scared he might not get down in time. I cannot remember the fire at all, but remember the long walk through the heather on Father's shoulders.

The family then moved to another house in Sutton where Ivan would live for the rest of his life:

> A surprise move was made in 1900 to Clapham Lodge, an old house with a two-acre garden in the middle of farmland, near Banstead Downs. We had to wait for water to be laid on and there was no proper sanitation, and no gas or electricity. I think we got the property from Mr Overton, the landowner, for the matter of a few hundred pounds.

Clapham Lodge was built in 1864 in the Georgian style for Miss Lucy Thornton. Her family had founded the 'Clapham Sect' who actively supported the ideas of William Wilberforce for the abolition of slavery in the early nineteenth century.

Ivan was educated at Sutton High School until he was 10 and then at County School, now Manor School, Sutton. At 12 years old, he joined the Boys' Life Brigade at Sutton Congregational Church. His brother Athel was captain at the time. He commented in an audio memoir: 'Our company of the BLB was the first thing of its kind in Sutton. The scouts weren't formed until 1907. It therefore attracted a lot of boys – thirty on the first night.' The first camp was in 1907 and his tent was under the charge of Sergeant Harry Daniels. Sadly, he would later photograph Daniels' war grave in 1916.

'We all enjoyed life at Clapham Lodge. I had a little tricycle I used to ride round the paths.' (Early 1900s.)

The BLB was founded in 1899 by the National Sunday School Union and was most prevalent in non-conformist churches. It followed the formation of the Boys' Brigade in 1883 by Sir William Alexander Smith, which sought to provide adolescent boys with the opportunity to engage in a range of activities, learn new skills, serve the community and grow in Christian discipleship. It was the Boys' Brigade movement that pioneered organized camping. Ivan found the BLB extremely beneficial, describing himself as 'timid and nervous – but a year or two in the Boys' Brigade gave me confidence.' By 1914 he became an officer and it would never cease to be a central part of his life.

Ivan in a darkroom at Kodak, c.1914.

I remained at school until I was 19 and passed the London Matriculation examination, and then I went to a Training School for Photograph Engraving and Lithography in London, and from there obtained a job as a laboratory assistant to Wratton and Wainright, [photographic] plate manufacturers at Croydon. That firm was bought up by Kodak Ltd and I therefore became employed by Kodaks where I remained working for 41 years.

Wratton and Wainright was the first company to manufacture dry plates for commercial use.

War Breaks Out

In 1914 rumours were flying about that there was a risk of war with Germany. The company [of the Boys Life Brigade] carried on until 1914 which was its last camp because the war broke out during the camp. We went to camp as usual with several London companies at Hythe on a rather nice field close to the railway station. We carried on the usual kind of programme and I took a lot of photos using a plate camera 6½ x 4¾ and developing in a portable darkroom on the field. I used to get a boy to bring me a bottle of cherry cider as a refresher. We were lucky to have Rev. E Pierce Powell with us as chaplain. On the Tuesday [4 August], I think it was, all our territorial officers including Athel, got a telegram calling them to report to their HQ. So on Wednesday morning we held a little farewell service in the camp with a skeleton staff (I was a Lieutenant at the time). We wished them Godspeed as we saw them off at the station. All that night troops were going off in trains from Hythe Station. After that there were more thrills and excitements as the war preparations were carried out, troops in training sometimes half the night through with their band playing, and when at last the end of our camp came on the Saturday, we had a very slow journey home being shunted into sidings to make room for troop trains passing us.

On return to normal life at Sutton I had to take over the captaincy and did my best to run an interesting programme for the boys, and we had a junior section called Cadets which I also ran. Oswald Stapley gave me a hand. Among my members was Phillip Evans a cadet of 11 years of age. We kept going until May 1915.

Athel had been serving in the Territorial Force since 1908, in the Royal Army Medical Corps, and received mobilization orders as soon as war broke out. He, like Ivan, was at the front until 1919, although very little material belonging to him survives beyond a few letters and his war medals. He is often mentioned in the diaries of Ivan and Viola.

Viola writes in August 1914:

> The mobilisation envelope came for Athel on August 5th and we had to telegraph to him at the BLB Camp. Mr Powell was down there and gave him a farewell service and then all the boys marched to the station to see him off, and half of them were crying. The next morning we said goodbye to him, thinking we should not see him again till the war was over. He looked so splendid in his uniform ready for active service. We each kissed him and then he went up the Avenue, his arm around Mother, while Father walked the other side of him. He told Father, who went a little way with him that this was going to make a man of him. He also asked that we should all remember him in prayer at a fixed hour every day, and he would do the same of us. However, that wasn't the last. He is still coming backwards and forwards from headquarters but each time we say goodbye it may be the last for a long time. He is to be inoculated against typhoid today and won't be back tonight for certain.

A postcard photograph of 'Captain at Crowborough', stamped 17 April 1915, sent by Ivan to Cadet Phillip Evans. He was referring to Corporal Athel Bawtree (centre) at his training camp standing casually with other RAMC comrades.

Viola was deeply shaken by the outbreak of war and plainly expressed her sentiments. However, her distress is mixed with glimmers of hope:

> How ghastly it all is. I feel as if we're all the victims of a nightmare. How can such things be real! Yet amidst all the horrible blackness there are beautiful rifts of light. Parliament is united at last. No more shameful squabblings about Home Rule. The Tories are loud in their praise of the Government. Everywhere hearts are being drawn together. Messages of fellowship come from all over the world

> and offers of help. Also such great trouble will make many men and women when the trouble becomes bigger and closer as it is sure to do. I do hope I'll come up to the scratch. I'm failing rottenly at present. I'm all on edge and the slightest thing annoys me. I must be a true woman at such a time. I'm praying to God that He will work a miracle and bring the war to a speedy end without much more bloodshed. There's no pleasure in reading of our enemy's defeat. It simply means more slaughter, more sorrowing widows and mothers. I never thought such an awful crisis could happen in modern times.

No 'speedy end' to the war was forthcoming and ten months later Ivan would also be heading to the Western Front. When war broke out he did not run to the nearest army

The photograph below is of the Bawtree family at Clapham Lodge, taken during the First World War. The exact date is unknown, and Ivan is missing, presumably because he was at the front at the time. Back row from left: Viola, Athel in uniform, Sylvia, unknown lady (an educated guess suggests this could be Milena Lilley, known as Aunt Millie), Lucy (née Legg) and Alfred Edwin (my great-grandparents). Sitting: Matilda and Alfred Bawtree. Kneeling: Elaine.

recruiting office like so many who were caught by the wave of patriotism that swept the nation at the time. When asked by two old army 'buffers' why he didn't join the army he replied that it was his duty to stay at home. There is no evidence that he had any conscientious objection to enlistment, so it seems that he simply felt that he should stay put. It is clear that he felt some level of duty to his family, as well as to the Boys' Life Brigade, given that Athel was already in the army, and we know from reading Viola's diaries that their father Alfred was suffering from deteriorating eyesight and financial problems. His eldest brother Alfred was already aged 40 with a young family in 1914. It is therefore likely that Ivan's parents were somewhat dependent on him, not to mention reluctant to wave goodbye to a second son heading off to the front.

In 1915 a golden opportunity arose for Ivan to go to France to use his professional skills in a non-combatant role. Pressure to sign up was mounting and by 1916 conscription was introduced which would almost certainly have ensured his enlistment. He recounted his own war service enlistment in his memoirs:

> As the war progressed I soon got involved. A special message came to Kodak Ltd, where I was working in Dept. 19 Technical Dept. under Jim Brown without much worry. I was approached by the managing director to know if I would take on a job for the BRCS in France to use a Kodak camera and take photos of the war graves. I consulted with them at home and it was agreed I should go, but mother wanted me not to take too great a risk because Athel also was in the forces. Well, of course, I just had to chance that. In 5 days I got my equipment, had injections, passport etc and within a week I was on my way to France.
>
> Returning for a moment to the BB, Laurence Pascall, a member of our church, took over the company but he himself joined the forces and the company was disbanded in September 1915.

The mammoth task of graves registration was started by Major Fabian Ware. He was too old at 45 to enlist in the army in 1914, but instead gained command of a mobile ambulance unit provided by the British Red Cross Society, initially helping to get wounded soldiers to Red Cross posts and hospitals. He soon realized that as the casualties were mounting up there was no official procedure for registering and marking the graves of those who had been killed. The British Expeditionary Force (BEF) was too poorly equipped to deal with grave registration on the scale required and couldn't have anticipated such huge casualties. Men were being buried in haphazard fashion amid chaotic situations, often by the roadside, right where they fell. Ware decided to start recording details of the graves so that the next of kin could be informed. The task of graves registration soon superseded the recovery of the wounded as Ware was under-resourced to keep up with both endeavours.

At first there was an apparent reluctance to direct funds towards an activity that did not directly help the war effort. However, by March 1915 General Sir Douglas Haig saw fit to write to the War Office:

> It is fully recognised that the work of this organisation is of purely sentimental value, and that it does not directly contribute to the successful termination of the war. It has, however, an extraordinary moral value to the Troops in the Field as well as to the relatives and friends of the dead at home. The mere fact that these officers visit day after day, the cemeteries close behind the trenches, fully exposed to shell and rifle fire, accurately to record not only the names of the dead but also the exact place of burial, has a symbolic value to the men that it would be difficult to exaggerate.
>
> It should be borne in mind that on termination of hostilities the nation will demand an account from the Government as to the steps which have been taken to mark and classify the burial places of the dead, steps which can only be effectively taken at, or soon after, burial.

The importance of Ware's work was finally recognized by the military authorities in March 1915 when the Graves Registration Commission came into being on the Western Front. It started as a Red Cross operation, supplied by the army.

The London branch of the Red Cross had created an Enquiry Department for the Wounded and Missing in late 1914, set up by Lord Robert Cecil. This was the only official avenue for relatives to pursue lines of enquiry about missing loved ones. Once the GRC got under way it was able to furnish Cecil's department with much more information. As the work of the GRC became more publicized, it was soon receiving numerous requests from distraught relatives desperate for information, photographs and details of the locations of the graves. By May 1915 Ware concluded that it therefore had become necessary for the GRC to seek out the services of a few professional photographers.

Since Ivan was working for Kodak at the time he was an obvious choice to recruit into Ware's mobile unit to help meet the public demand for information about the fallen. One of his colleagues, Frederick Roper, had also been recruited. This was pioneering work as never before had such attention been given to military war dead and the needs of their relatives.

Ivan's diary from 1915 details his calling to go to Flanders to work for the GRC:

28.5.15 Mr Hear mentions temporary job of photographer in GRC in Flanders. Obtain consent of Father and Mother.

29.5.15 Interview [with] Lieut. Brook in reception hall at Kodaks. Mentions screw [wage] as 30/- per week, gives particulars of work and mentions that we are liable to shell-fire but that we never have to work under rifle fire or in places which are known to be regularly shelled. Afterwards interview [with] Mr Mathisson. Nothing definite fixed up.

31.5.15 Receive letter instructing to go up to Pall Mall and suggesting Tuesday as a suitable day for departure. Visit Pall Mall 11pm. See Mr Hastings. Rush back to Sutton and try and get various doctors' signatures for passport. Finally get Dr Morgan's. Reach Pall Mall 3pm and go through many wearisome performances in which I am accompanied by Roper – the other photographer obtained from Kodaks. Roper had been taking photos in S. Africa. Interview by two old Buffers and asked why I don't join the army. Told them I felt it was my duty to stay at home. They fight it out between themselves and the Doctor passes and inoculates. Go round to uniform dept. and get served out with full equipment but no mess-tin or anything of that kind. Get down to Cadets Parade, say goodbye and dismiss them. Stapley agrees to take over the Cadets and to help with the company.

1.6.15 Again visit Pall Mall and go through other processes towards getting a passport. Have to wait an hour or two in RAC entrance hall for signature of Secretary of BRCS. Visit Kodaks and say goodbye to J.B. and others. C. Bumm gives me the photograph of Sapper Grayling, the first Kodak boy to be killed, and asks me to look up the grave if I ever visit Armentières.

2.6.15 Go up to London and receive railway ticket. We are to catch the 8.30 boat-train to Folkestone on Thursday. Get home and make hurried preparations. Take BLB parade and say goodbye to boys. Say goodbye to VAD and the NCOs. Pack kitbag.

Arrival in France

3.6.15 Get up at 5.30 and finish packing kit. Say goodbye to family and cycle off to Sutton where Mr Lawton accompanied me to Victoria, travelled down with

Lord Londsdale. Victoria the train leaves. Reached Folkestone about 11. As we pass Sandling Junction could not help thinking of the last time I was there – taking the boys home from the Hythe camp. Reached Folkestone and got out on the pier where we hung about until we could get our passports viséed. At last we get onto our boat which leaves at about 11.30. Very very strange it was seeing the white cliffs slowly receding. Had a fine view of Hythe and Sandgate (the first view from the sea). The little steamer we were on got up a fine speed and the crossing was very enjoyable.

The sea was as smooth as glass. We had not been going for long when a torpedo destroyer appeared on the scene and convoyed us for a mile or two. Then on the left we saw a long line of buoys stretching out to sea. These buoys support a big net which prevents submarines from getting through. It was only half completed when I crossed. After about a couple of hours (during which I succeeded in smoking a cigarette) we sighted the French coast – very pretty with little red tiled roofs dotted about on the hills. Outside Boulogne we reversed and went into the

Boulogne Harbour. Boulogne was one of the three main Channel ports through which British soldiers would enter and leave France during the war. It would have been a hive of activity, with the constant movement of supplies, fresh or returning troops, soldiers going on leave, and the wounded. It also had a large rest camp which Ivan had to use on a few occasions, several base hospitals and of course a military cemetery.

harbour stern foremost. There was a good deal of shipping in the harbour and three large hospital ships. We landed and made our way along the quay and over the river to the Hotel Christol – the headquarters of the BRCS. Here we reported and were sent round to dinner at the Café Christol – a dirty little café in a side street. We arrived in Boulogne about 1.30.

We had a good dinner, veal, potatoes and beans and then went back to the Hotel C where we expected a car from Major Ware's unit. No car had come so we went for a walk in the town.

The quay and main streets were very busy and full of English soldiers. Running alongside the quay was a special barricaded road for the sole use of the ambulances. All the roads are roughly cobbled (pavée). While we were on the quay a big convoy of ambulances came down the road – all full of wounded. Serious cases were carried very slowly and gently. This procession crossed the bridge and drew up alongside the hospital ships. There they were unloaded and carried onto the ships. There were over a hundred ambulances. We saw a hospital nurse carried on board too. We strolled back to the Hotel and were told that we should be fetched the following morning as our car had broken down.

We took our kit and went round to Café Christol where I bagged a bed in the front room. There was an old billiard table at the café but everything was pretty nearly broken up. After tea we went for another walk and visited the older part of the town, situated at the top of the hill and surrounded by a thick wall. Then we went round to the Salvation Army next and had some fruit and listened to the piano they had. It was a very pleasant evening.

Turned into the billet about 10 o'clock. Just as we were thinking of undressing, one of the fellows broke the gas mantle so we were obliged to go to bed in the dark. There were a lot of fellows there quite sick of the place – they had been in 15 days without work to do – besides whitewashing the walls of the billet. I did not sleep that night what with the cats and novelty of the situation.

4.6.15 In the morning we left the Hotel and met Dewdney who told us to meet him at 3pm. At 3 o'clock we got the Delawny bus and went round to the [page torn] for one or two hours. Here we met Fuggles and Walsh in the ambulance and were told to transfer to the ambulance as that would take us back. The ambulance had come down that afternoon carrying a chap suffering from appendicitis. Fuggles and Walsh seemed fairly decent fellows and gave us amusing accounts of Lillers and life there. At last at 5 o'clock we were off and up the hill. It was jolly cold and misty in Boulogne when we left. At the top of the hill we passed the barrier and

Boulogne Harbour. If the camera was to pan 90 degrees to the right, the Hotel Christol would come into view.

were well on our way to Lillers. We came via Aire etc. and had a good run up hill and down hill and round sharp corners at a fine old lick. After we had been going for about an hour the weather turned much warmer and the sun came out. About half way we stopped at a wayside café and had drinks. I had café noir.

We arrived at Lillers and drove up the avenue of Poplars, turned into the gateway, rounded the bend and there we were. We arrived just in time for dinner. The mess-room was a kind of cellar under the main hall of the Château Relingue and when we entered it, it was full of the men all sitting round the table. I was welcomed by Bert Haddon, a tall chap who had been a chemist salesman at

One of Ivan's postcards of the Château de Relingue.

> Amersham and had dabbled in photography a bit. There was no place for us but Haddon made room for us and we had a good dinner. Roper and I turned into an ambulance and fixed ourselves up on stretchers but we got jolly cold by the morning. That night the guns were going like anything and we heard them for we lay awake with the cold.

The wounded being transported to the hospital ships in Boulogne were most likely to have been casualties of the Second Battle of Ypres which had concluded on 25 May 1915. This battle saw one of the first large-scale deployments of poison gas and sadly would have provided plenty of work for Ivan's introduction to the Western Front.

Chapter Two

The Graves Registration Unit

The First World War saw unprecedented casualties from an army that had been massively increased by volunteers from the civilian population and by conscripts from January 1916 onwards. In previous wars it was normal to bury dead soldiers in mass graves; only those of higher rank could expect to have their own personal grave or memorial. However, in the First World War this all changed and it was decided that each soldier, regardless of rank, should be given an individual burial

GR Unit in a Ford car, Ypres. The cross standing behind the car has the name of Private A.C. Pike, AIF (Australian Imperial Force) written on it. Curiously, current records show that his name is inscribed on the Menin Gate, implying that he has no known grave.

with a wooden cross, later to be replaced with a headstone. Naturally this required a much more meticulous level of organization to accurately record the details of fallen soldiers and the location of their graves so that as many men as possible could be accounted for, and as much information as possible could be provided to relatives.

By May 1915, as the work of the GRC continued to grow, Ware realized that a photographic department was becoming increasingly necessary to meet the public demand for information. On 21 May Lieutenant Charles T. Wilson of the GRC drafted a 'Scheme for founding a Section for dealing with enquiries for Graves and applications for Photographs.' The following is an excerpt from it:

> In the districts now occupied by the British Army the graves are very frequently grouped in large numbers in cemeteries and burial grounds and a large number could be taken in course of a day's work. There are also Cemeteries close to Base Hospitals where the graves are close together in a particular part of the cemetery where a large number could also be taken in a day's work. Some of these Cemeteries, however, are situate in widely different parts of France. From information already received by the GRC from 3rd Echelon it would appear that there are graves as far south as Nantes. There are also many graves situate so close to the actual seat of hostilities that it would not always be possible, or if possible perhaps not desirable, to take photographs of them or such photographs could only be taken at particular times.
>
> Having regard to these difficulties I would suggest that, at the outset, not more than three competent photographers should be employed solely for the purpose of taking photographs. They should, in the first instance, devote as much of their time as possible to taking collective photographs of Cemeteries and groups of graves as suggested by the Memorandum of the A.G. dated 3/4/15. I take it that this Memorandum suggests as a wise course to follow that photographs of all the graves in a particular group should be taken even though a few only may have been applied for at the time of taking them, as it may reasonably be expected that, when this department of GRC work is better known to the public, photographs of many other graves in the same group will be applied for and a suitable index of negatives could easily be arranged to provide for such future applications.

Ivan's job was therefore initially to photograph as many graves as possible, but he would find that his workflow broadened to other activities such as clerical work and making crosses as at times the military situation or weather conditions would preclude photographic excursions.

At first, graves registration was carried out by the Mobile Unit that Ware had created in 1914. Ivan describes it in his diary from 14 August 1915:

> Will take this opportunity in describing the mobile unit. This was a hospital unit of the BRCS and was attached to the French. It did splendid work at Arras and collected men right from the trenches. For the work it did both Major Ware and Dr Kelly received the Legion of Honour and the military medal on behalf of the unit. Then the hospital was given up and the GRC work taken over. Haddon obtained his reputation as a photographer by making some good photographs for passports. His real work was a dispenser at the Pharmacy Waldorfe. Major Ware interviewed him and the photographer job was started.

A small brass plaque that was among Ivan's photographs. This was the method of marking graves in the early days, before wooden crosses were used.

Ivan described the work as it got under way in his memoirs and 1915 diary:

> In France at first we travelled in an officer's car to various cemeteries: Bailleul, Bethune, Ypres, Kemmel etc. but as more and more work came in we went for several weeks and stayed at a Graves Registration Section. There we had a number of these: Bailleul, Poperinghe, Estaires, Amiens, Arras, Dunkirk, Dickebusch etc. From those sections we got a lift in a car when possible but otherwise carried our equipment on our backs and rode a push bike. The more formal cemeteries were

reached first by car and then on foot through communication trenches etc. Quite an adventure and a certain amount of shelling as we worked close by some of our batteries. It was not always funny.

5.6.15 Introduced to Mr Wilson who describes how the graves are photographed and recorded. Generally, about 5 graves are taken on each film and each film is autographed with a serial number and the photographer's own letter (A for Haddon, B for Wilson, C for Roper and D for me). In describing any particular grave afterwards it is spoken of say 3 L-R or R-L as the case may be. Haddon showed us the darkroom and we examined our cameras etc. Haddon had his bed in the darkroom and we kept all our kit there too.

Roper and Haddon went off to Choques, a small village about halfway between us and Bethune and I went with Mr Wilson and McDonnell and Rateau in the Rover car to Locre cemetery via Bailleul. To get to Bailleul you pass through Merville which is reached either by a narrow little road or by a very rough road alongside the canal. Before turning off on either way there is a good stretch of about 5km on good pavée to St Venant. The roads are lined all the way with lorries carrying supplies and ammunition. Just after St Venant you have to pass over the canal on a drawbridge and a French soldier stops you and requires to see your pass. Merville is a fair sized place with narrow streets all leading to the central market square in front of the church.

From Merville the road to Bailleul is fairly decent. In several places along the road signs of the German retreat (from Paris) can be observed. Cottages burnt to the ground or very much damaged and just outside an inn a British soldier's grave. As you go into Bailleul you pass the remains of a house where a Zeppelin bomb fell during a raid in the winter.

Bailleul is an interesting place though rather dirty and possesses a fine town hall in front of which is the usual pavée square. Almost immediately opposite the town hall the Rue d'Armentières turns off. Down here on the right is the GRC 'B' section's headquarters, a very ordinary house.

The organisation of the GRC is as follows. A Section is at Bethune and is responsible for finding out, recording and marking all graves in La Bassée and that district. B Section is at Bailleul and is responsible for Kemmel to Armentières places of burial. C Section is at Poperinghe and is responsible for the Ypres and northern part of the line. D Section is responsible for the Marne and the Aisne and has its headquarters at Compiegne and La Feurty [*sic* – probably La Ferté]. There is also a section at Amiens to which the British have now extended their

Bailleul Grande Place, completely destroyed by the end of the war.

line. All these sections send in reports to the HQ at Lillers and the reports are typed out and put in a gigantic card index.

We did not stop long in Bailleul but were soon off to Locre. On the way we passed a big asylum now used as a hospital and on one side of this was a big flying ground. The country here is a bit more hilly and just over the Belgian frontier there is a good big rise. At the top of this rise is the village of Locre. We did not stop at the cemetery but went on a little way to the brow of the hill and had lunch.

From this position the ruined tower of Ypres could be seen in the distance. No bombardment was taking place that day so it just showed up as a ruined tower. This is the place from which the Prime Minister viewed Ypres. We then returned to Locre Cemetery and I exposed 40 or 50 negatives. Rateau and I went back to Bailleul in a rattly old steam lorry and nearly got shaken to death. About a dozen French boys climbed up behind while we were going along and had a joy ride.

6.6.15 I took a walk with Lieut. Wilson through the woods to Equedeck [Ecquedecques]. Near the church in a field are the graves of two soldiers who

Bailleul Asylum.

died accidentally through sleeping too near a charcoal fire. I photographed these and we returned to Lillers. In the afternoon we had a rest. In the evening Father Waggett conducted a short service in the office.

7.6.15 Mr Plummer drives us in an ambulance to Merville Cemetery which we reach via the canal. A boiling hot day and a very dusty dry cemetery with big mounds of earth half covering the graves. We were glad to get back into the shelter of the car.

8.6.15 to 13.6.15 Stay at Lillers and develop and help in the office.

14.6.15 Go to Bailleul via Aire with Lieut. Wilson and Haddon. Finish a few rows in Bailleul Old Cmty, have tea at the Section and return to Lillers in time for dinner.

15.6.15 Go to Bailleul with Wall and Haddon and photograph a good many graves in Bailleul annex. The flying ground was quite near the cemetery and many aeroplanes passed over. On our way back I notice an 85th Field Ambulance van and on enquiry find that the driver knows Athel very well and has been out shopping only that afternoon. He gives me directions how to find the Château Mont Noire and I leave a message for Athel to the effect I shall probably look in on the following day.

16.6.15 Haddon and I pack up our beds and in the afternoon Lieut. Wilson takes us over to our Section at Bailleul where we are to stay for a day or two. By the time we get over there it is too late to call on Athel but Lieut. Wilson makes arrangements for a visit on the following day. We make acquaintance with the section and plant our beds in one of the bedrooms where Hopkins, Austin, Heading and Handley slept. Then have a jolly good dinner in the kitchen and go to bed.

At 5.30 we got up and are at work in the cemetery by 6am, taking those crosses which face east. After breakfast we work in the cemetery all the morning and part of the afternoon. At 5 o'clock Handley takes me up the road towards Locre and we search for the Château Mont Noire. We pass Locre and turn off the La Clytte route to Westoutre. From Westoutre we go straight up the hill and past the windmill and find the Château gates on the left.

On enquiring I am told that Corporal Bawtree is in and I make my way down the beautiful avenue towards the Château. Just before getting to the Château I meet Sergt. Greenslade looking very brown and well. The last time I saw him was at the summer camp. After a short chat with him he directs me to go past the Château and down the grassy slope where I shall find Athel rigging up a clothes line under a clump of trees. Sure enough there he was and we shook hands and he showed me round the place. Then we went on top of the hill where we were able to get a grand view of the plain of Flanders. Athel pointed out all the places of interest to me. Then we said goodbye and I was off again on the ambulance. Arrived back in good time for dinner.

20.6.15 Dr Boswell takes me to Hazebrouck with Seward. The road to Hazebrouck is much the same as the others in the neighbourhood but from one point a very good view of the surrounding manufacturing country can be obtained. I hunted round the old cemetery and found the one grave which had to be done and then spent the remainder of the day helping Dr Boswell to put up crosses. Hazebrouck new cemetery is a brick-field next to the old cemetery and a very dirty place altogether. I was glad when we finished and went off home. In the evening Father Waggett conducted a service in the office as before.

21.6.15 Go to St Omer with Lieut. Wilson and after calling on the A.G. and one or two other places, make our way to the cemetery. Before entering the town we had to show a pass at the barrier and the same applied to leaving the town. The Souvenir Cemetery lies on top of a hill overlooking the town of which a good view is obtained. In the town are many fashionable shops and houses and two fine churches.

We photographed nearly all the cemetery and then cut off home where we arrived just in time for dinner. The journey only took ¾ hour so we must have exceeded the limit part of the way.

22.6.15 to 26.6.15 Spend at Lillers in developing and assisting in the office.

27.6.15 Go to St Omer with Lieut. Hamilton, Mr McDonnell, and Gunning, and finish the Souvenir Cemetery barring a few new graves. Have ½ hour to look round the town. Go into the church which is not so old inside as out. The inside is very fine and gaudy but quite new. The organ is magnificent and is like a bridge right across the back of the church.

28.6.15 to 4.7.15 Spend at Lillers as usual. Will try and describe the place better now. The groundsheets for making Kodak House were obtained from the Staff

Souvenir Cemetery, overlooking the town of St Omer.

Sergt. of the next door camp which was the Highland Casualty Clearing Station. Before we lived in the Kodak House we used to wash in the stream just outside the château. Can describe place at Lillers better at some other time, but have already described it in previous letters.

5.7.15 Go to Vieille Chapelle with Lieut. Wilson but it came on to drizzle so we had to abandon the work. To get to V. Chapelle you go to Bethune and then turn to the left over the canal. The road to Bethune is pretty good pavée lying between an avenue of trees all of the same height (just like all French trees seem to be). About ½ way you pass through the village of Choques which is not worthy of any particular mention. Near Bethune there is a big coal mine and a tall mine shaft arrangement which shows up for miles round. The section at Bethune is down a little side street on the Choques side of town. Many houses in the town are knocked about especially towards the other side. From Bethune we went to Vieille Chapelle. This is a very small village but has been badly knocked about and the church consists of only a low brick wall and a heap of blackened masonry.

There were a lot of Indians encamped round the place. The military cemetery is in a field just outside the village. The graves are in an orchard and are beautifully looked after. Drizzle coming on we had to abandon our day's work.

6.7.15 Go to Vieille Chapelle with Haddon and Wall in an ambulance. On the way from Bethune to VC we have a tyre burst but soon fix a new wheel. While having lunch at VC we see a lot of practice in the neighbouring field with hand grenades.

Then we heard a noise like stout calico being torn followed by a bang. This was a village being shelled about ½ mile away. (I believe it was Laventie.) Having finished Vieille Chapelle which contains a lot of Indian officers' graves we made our way to Estaires. On the way I noticed a church with just the clock blown out of the spire. It looked very curious. I also noticed the front of a white house which was absolutely riddled with shrapnel. We did some work in Estaires cemetery, had our dinner and went along the road we had come by to La Gorgue, a typical French cemetery. This we entirely cleared up. Then we went back to Lillers after a rather good day's work.

Vieille Chapelle Churchyard Cemetery. The cross on the left marks the grave of Gunner F. Grethe of the 10th Siege Battery, Royal Garrison Artillery, killed in action on 23 May 1915. After the armistice the graves were transferred to larger cemeteries.

7.7.15 to 11.7.15 Stopped at Lillers in office etc. About this time Roper went down south to photograph graves on the Marne.

12.7.15 Go with Lieut Wilson and Haddon to Armentières via Bethune and Lestrem. In Lestrem were a few memorials of men who had fallen and been buried at Neuve Chapelle. These I photographed. Then we made our way to Cité Bon Jean (Armentières) where we did a good bit of work and then returned. Met the Rev. Webb-Peploe just outside Armentières.

13.7.15 to 20.7.15 Stop at Lillers as usual. Receive a small part of the goods ordered from London in the middle of June, but no Velox paper or acid hypo. Find all the goods are ordered through Fallowfield. Lieut Wilson leaves for the Marne to join Roper.

21.7.15 Go out with new boss Mr McDonnell and Hudd to Cité Bon Jean via Sailly Sur Lys. At the latter place there is a cemetery named cemetery post. Here we photographed one grave and then pushed on to Cité Bon Jean which we finished. Then we went through Armentières to Nieppe where we found one grave. We came back through Bailleul where we had tea. Found Sapper Grayling's grave at Cité Bon Jean.

22.7.15 Make our first batch of prints with the Velox paper just arrived. Tone and glaze and finish them. C.O. very pleased with the result.

23.7.15 Haddon goes on leave, Handley sleeps in the hut with me and a dog also passes the night with us.

24.7.15 Go to Hinges cemetery (near Bethune) with Mr McDonnell. While in Bethune hear six shells come over. Find out afterwards that 12 men have been killed and 30 injured on the other side of the town by these. Hinges is a funny little cemetery enclosed by a white fence in a corn field on top of a hill overlooking Bethune. Photograph a few graves there and come along home.

25.7.15 Make 30 or 40 prints and develop both Haddon's and my own negatives.

26.7.15 Go to Locre and Dranoutre via Bailleul with Mr McDonnell. On the way we are rather startled by things bursting and sending out clouds of smoke in

Grande Place, Béthune, 1919. The belfry, built in 1346, was still standing, although the uppermost section, which included the fifteenth-century wooden spire, was blown away.

a corn field by the side of the road but find they are only trench mortars or hand grenades which our men are practicing with.

From Bailleul we make our way to Locre. As we go up the hill one of the sausages (captive balloons) [used for observation to find suitable targets and estimate the range for the artillery] is just being raised near the side of the road. I wonder to myself whether the Germans will try conclusions with it. Retake various graves in Locre churchyard. While doing so a noise like stout calico being torn is heard and then a big bang and a puff of yellow smoke up in the air but not very near the balloon. Then a lot more German shells come over but all fall short of the mark and uncomfortably close to the road we have to go back by. Having finished Locre we make our way back and hold our breath (so to speak) while we pass under the balloon, which we notice is being drawn down. See a soldier returning with some pieces of shell which he has succeeded in digging out.

Have our lunch by the roadside and then finish Dranoutre cemetery and make off to Lillers. On the way back to Lillers I noticed a lot of funny little mushroom clouds in strings across the sky. On enquiry I found that this was shrapnel bursting round an aeroplane which I could just see as a black speck moving swiftly along. First there was a bright flash like the sun catching on a mirror then the puff of smoke appeared. These little puffs of smoke followed the aeroplane as it went. It was a very strange sight.

27.7.15 Develop previous day's negs and then go to Pont Nieppe via Bailleul with Mr McDonnell and McKay (one of the clerks). On the way to Pont Nieppe we pass an engineers camp and see protective canvas being prepared. This canvas is used for making huts and is painted over with splashes and blotches of green, yellow and red to make it look like part of the country when viewed from above. Near the camp was an anti-aircraft gun and another captive balloon not far from the road.

At Pont Nieppe we photograph the graves and then returned to Bailleul Cemetery where we did one or two odd graves. On the way to Bailleul we again saw an aeroplane being shelled. At Bailleul we photographed one or two graves and then returned to Lillers.

28.7.15 Go to La Clytte Cemetery via Bailleul and Locre. Very clear day after the rain and get a magnificent view of Ypres from Locre Hill. We (Mr McDonnell and I) do a lot of graves, which are very well kept here, and get off home. There is a big gun on the hill near La Clytte and every now and then it would give us an exhibition of its properties.

29.7.15 Went to Kemmel with Mr McDonnell via Bailleul and La Clytte. Arrived at La Clytte we finished the work there and then went onto Kemmel. The road to Kemmel branches off the Ypres road just past La Clytte. We had not got far up the Kemmel road before we noticed dugouts and trenches in great profusion on each side of the road. This indicated the presence of our batteries. A dug-out proper is a protected hide hole with a roof but the trenches are used for the same purpose i.e. protection from shells. They are very narrow and are lined with sandbags. Of course there was no sign of the guns themselves but they kept on firing.

Presently we came to a barrier and a sentry on guard. Here we left the car and travelled in to the town on foot. At the side of the road was a ditch running under the hedge and all foot traffic had to travel along this as they might be visible on the road. On the next hill top we could just see a stretch of barren brown earth which marked the German lines. Kemmel was entirely in ruins – although it seemed only a small place. The houses were torn all to pieces but, strange to say, the church appeared practically undamaged externally. Passing through the village we turned to the left beside a wood in which I noticed some dug-outs. Then we came to the beautiful cemetery on the right. At the corner of this cemetery was a shrine grotto built into an old hollow tree. As we passed through the village everything was deadly silent except for a gun firing every now and then, but this seemed to intensify the silence.

We met a party of men just returned from the trenches and scarcely had enough energy to salute properly. Further on we met two staff officers who returned our salute and said good morning. The cemetery itself was beautifully kept and all the graves planted with flowers. It was quite a pleasure to photograph the graves. We had not been working there long when – bang – off went a gun immediately behind us in the wood and we heard the shell tearing its way through the air and finally bursting where it landed in the German lines. It made me jump. And the second time they fired it was almost worse for I was anticipating it.

The man in charge of the cemetery (a soldier) showed us and made Mr McDonnell a present of a large splinter of shell which had burst only a few yards from him while he was standing near a certain oak tree which he pointed out in the next field. Having photographed all the officers' graves we returned through

Dedication ceremony at Bailleul British Military Cemetery, on All Saints' Day (1 November) 1915. Three British army chaplains lead the assembled officers and men in a hymn. Nurses can be seen standing behind the soldiers on the left-hand side.

the village, had a look round the churchyard for any other graves. We noticed a big hole where a shell had entered the side of the church but that was all the damage done. The houses all around were practically razed to the ground, but such as were left standing were inhabited by the villagers. It is a marvel how these people stick it.

On the way back we noticed a woman and child walking along the road so we followed their example and did not take to the ditch. We took the car ½ mile back along the road and had our lunch. While sitting in the car I noticed an arc of flame leap out of a bush in the neighbouring field. It must have been 6 to 10 feet long and several feet wide. After about 10 seconds we heard a big bang and the noise of the shell. This was one of our batteries in action. The flashes and bangs kept on coming. Sometimes two or three at a time. Lunch finished we returned home via Bailleul (it was 4.15 before we started lunch).

Three tall splintered trees and a view of Kemmel from Locre.

30.7.15 Develop spools and make one or two prints. Mr McDonnell tells me that he really ought not to have taken me to Kemmel as I am not supposed to visit such places. At 9.30pm Haddon returns from leave.

1.8.15 Roper and Lieut. Wilson return from Compiegne. We hear that Mr Wilson is being taken off the photography job.

2.8.15 Spend the most objectionable day I have had out here. Roper is a difficult man to get on with under ordinary circumstances but this day he excelled himself – grumbling and swearing at everything and everybody and letting me have the full benefit of it. I was helping him develop his spools. Haddon was out photographing.

3.8.15 to 5.8.15 Work in the office filing all day.

6.8.15 Go to Bailleul Cemetery with Roper and do ½ day's work. Part of the time we have to shelter under the porch of a French tomb. Some of these tombs have a complete little chapel over them and are got up in a most gorgeous and expensive style. I hear that a 17 inch shell has been dropped on the aviation ground by the Bailleul asylum and has killed 3 or 4 men. One noticeable feature of the roads out here is the little wayside shrines and crosses which you meet every few miles and at cross roads and prominent places. They are generally surrounded by a few straggling trees. The shrines have a kind of rack at the side which is full of small wooden crosses, evidently gifts to the shrine but I know not with what object. The wayside crosses are sometimes 20 feet high. There is a shrine at the corner of one of the ruined houses on the way to Bailleul. It is absolutely undamaged. I find out on the following day that Athel was in Bailleul having a look round only that afternoon. What a pity we didn't know.

8.8.15 Do some work in Bethune Cemetery and photograph the graves of the Inniskillings [Royal Inniskilling Fusiliers] who were killed by the shells I heard bursting the other day. Some of them were killed in their sleep. From Bethune we go to Hinges and take a general view of the little cemetery.

13.8.15 Get up early in the morning and see Mr McDonnell off as he goes off to Ireland for good. He was a quaint old boy but we liked him very well. He was giving up because he was tired with the unbusinesslike way the job was being run.

15.8.15 Lot of parcels and letters arrive. Work in the office all day. Have concert with whistle pipes and buzzers in Kodak house in the evening.

16.8.15 Print all day.

17.8.15 Set out for Dickebusch but only get as far as Bailleul owing to thunderstorm. Make about 3 exposures and then give up.

18.8.15 Work in office all day. Wet day.

19.8.15 All morning in office, afternoon printing.

20.8.15 Go to Dickebusch and Reninghelst via Bailleul and Locre. Dickebusch is really only a little way down the road from La Clytte. It is terribly bashed about and only about 2 houses were left standing. In these, however, the people were still living. The cemetery itself is just up against the worst of the ruins –

View of the church at Reninghelst. Wooden crosses can be seen in the churchyard. By the time Ivan took this photograph the place was certainly not 'untouched' as there is plenty of visible damage, although mild compared to many other places in this sector.

though it lies a few hundred feet away clear. But I should not care to be working in it during a bombardment. We just took the requests and then made our way to Reninghelst about 3 miles away. (Dickebusch is the town where Angel was quartered a few weeks ago [Angel's connection to Ivan is unknown; he was presumably a friend from home].) Reninghelst was quite a peaceful place and entirely untouched. We finished up the cemetery there and made our way back via West-Outre. This should have taken us right past Athel's Château but unluckily the road from West-Outre was under repair and we had to go back via Locre after all.

21.8.15 Develop. Send note to Athel by Chatwin.

22.8.15 Go to a morning service at No. 6 Casualty Clearing Station in the town. Good hymns but poor service C of E. A lot of wounded and 3 hospital nurses were present.

23.8.15 Print all day.

24.8.15 Very slack day. Deputy Adjutant General inspects the place.

25.8.15 Go to Poperinghe and Vlamertinghe via Hazebrouck. Start out with Roper, Haddon and myself but drop Roper at Hazebrouck cemetery. Then we make our way to Steenwerk and on to Poperinghe. Just outside Hazebrouck our tyre goes flat but that only delays us 10 minutes. Notice the effect of shells and bombs at Steenvoorde. Should have thought it was too far back for shells. Then pass through the town of Abeele and on to Poperinghe. The road to Poperinghe passes along the north side of the range of hills where the Château de Mont Noire and Mont des Cats is. I could just see the town where Angel is quartered. Poperinghe is quite a large place. As we entered it I noticed the effect of shrapnel in various places but only houses here and there were wrecked. Many houses were chipped, riddled and scarred by the bullets. We turned round by the church which was only slightly damaged and then turned to the left and stopped at Section C. Rather a nice little house with tiled floors and all very clean. Out at the back was a small garden with a pear tree in it. This was terminated by a 6 foot wall which supports the garden from a field.

When they shell Poperinghe (which they do about daily) the shells come over the house and drop in the field beyond. They are generally 6.9 inch and do not do any damage although so frequent. They sent some 17 inch over one week but they all fell in a field outside the town fortunately. There are several cemeteries at Poperinghe where most of the Ypres killed are buried. I photographed Rewcastle's grave (an O.S.). The old cemetery had a big hole in the wall where a shell had popped in. [Driver Donald Rewcastle, RAMC, died on 24 April 1915 and was buried in Poperinghe Old Military Cemetery.] From Poperinghe we went to Elverdinghe and then to Hospital Farm. This was a kind of rest camp. The men all lived in dug-outs which looked very comfortable but I shouldn't care to be in them in wet weather. There was a nice little cemetery in a field here and we finished it. On the way out the M.P. at the gate stopped us and asked what we were doing with cameras. We straightaway showed him our passes (both kinds) but he tried to be nasty even then, though with no success.

We then made our way to Vlamertinghe, a nasty bashed place similar to Dickebusch but we passed it on the outskirts and stopped at a place called Hop-Store where there was a nice little cemetery. As the time was getting on we were only able to photograph just the one request. Then we went off up the Poperinghe road. As we left Vlamertinghe we heard a shell burst in the town. Leaving Poperinghe we went home via Hazebrouck where we picked up Roper.

Poperinghe Old Military Cemetery which was used for burials from the First Battle of Ypres in October 1914 until the second battle in May 1915. Imprinted zinc strips can be seen on these tarred wooden crosses, designed to be as durable as possible in wet conditions.

Vlamertinghe, which lies between Poperinghe and Ypres. The military cemetery lies to the right of the church as viewed in this photograph.

Hop Store Cemetery, Vlamertinghe. The nearest grave on the left is that of Private Walter Ashworth of the Loyal North Lancashire Regiment, killed in action on 8 June 1917.

26.8.15 Develop negatives and take photograph of Mr Plummer in front of the château towers.

27.8.15 Go for a walk with Hammond at 6.15am to the hills past Equedeck. Go to St Omer see huge airship shed disguised as a haystack with painted canvas just like stage scenery. Finish off Souvenir Cemetery and return to Lillers. We develop in the afternoon. Mr Wilson visits Lillers.

29.8.15 Slack morning. Print in afternoon.

30.8.15 Finish off prints in the morning and then read for remainder of morning. Take photograph of Kodak House in the afternoon. Camera is smuggled up disguised as a soap box. Sergt. Comfort presses the button. Wash illicit film at night under spring and young RAMC fellow mentions that he only joined the army 10 days ago without any training and here he is on the job.

Ivan, Haddon and Roper outside their improvised darkroom, 'Kodak House', in the grounds of Château de Relingue, Lillers.

31.8.15 Tuesday work in office in morning, print in afternoon. Haddon and Roper go to Poperinghe district. Roper to Vlamertinghe and Haddon to Ypres. While Roper is at work shells come over in the next field. Immediately one of the fellows from the Hop Store runs out in search of souvenirs. While Haddon is at Ypres some 17 inch shells come over. He is shown a telegram which arrived some minutes before the 1st shell saying German heavies about to fire. This is a good example of the excellence of our intelligence system.

1.9.15 Slack day. Market day in Lillers.

2.9.15 Work in office all day.

3.9.15 Horrible wet day. So into town and buy books and read all the morning. Print in afternoon. Am told my leave is to take place on the 13th.

4.9.15 Slack day. Go to pictures in Lillers theatre at 4pm. Quite a good show under Pathé Frères. Lantern worked from the dynamo of a travelling ASC workshop. Several London Scottish came in. They are billeted in a village near Lillers.

5.9.15 Slack day. Football match in the afternoon (early morning walk to baths).

6.9.15 Roper goes on leave. After breakfast Haddon goes off to Bailleul for a week. Work in office and try to fit stove in the afternoon.

7.9.15 Early morning walk to Equideck [sic] with Hammond who tells how the unit got a Legion of Honour. Also mentions the case of a man who was wounded by the bones of the man next to him who was blown to pieces with a hand grenade. Work in Lillers Cemetery all day.

8.9.15 Work in Lillers cemetery and develop in the morning. Go out with Dr Boswell in the afternoon to Merville etc. Take a few graves at Merville and then go on to St Omer via Hazebrouck. See a battery of 12 inch guns drawn by caterpillars. Beautiful fine afternoon and jolly pretty country from Merville to Hazebrouck. Just as we came into Arques we had to wait ¼ hour for a long artillery column of the Canadians to pass us. In St Omer we visit the A.G.'s office and then some shops. Dr Boswell presents us with a nice pear and a newspaper to read. We come back via Aire.

10.9.15 Develop. Go to pictures with Gunning and Tyrrell in evening.

12.9.15 Go (by kind permission of Sgt. Hammond) to Mont Noir via Bailleul. He is really going to Poperinghe but agrees to drop me at Mt. Noir. There is a good bit of controversy as to the route to be followed. Finally it is decided to proceed via St Jean Capelle. After much climbing we reach the top of the hill and try and get up to the château gates but are stopped and asked for a pass. As we have not [got] one we very nearly decide to abandon my project (which was to see Athel). But I went up to the sentry and told him my reason for wishing to go up to the gates. He said you can go up if you want to but you would never come back. It appears that they were experimenting with a gun on the top of the hill and during the hour they were working the road was stopped. Then I make enquiries and find that the Château can be approached through the woods a little lower down the hill. I made arrangements with the car to meet me just outside a little cottage. They did not expect to get back there for an hour or two.

I made my way through the woods and at last arrived at the château and found Athel by his bivouac. He was pleased to see me. The experiment on the hill appeared to be firing shrapnel at various ranges on to concrete beds – a weird idea. On two occasions they pointed the gun the wrong way and shells burst in the open space in front of the château though nobody got hurt. Athel had to go through a short spell of physical drill under Sgt. Greenslade and then he and I were both invited to dinner by the brothers Hart. We had stewed rabbit (caught in the woods), dumpling and potatoes with some cake to follow. Then I went down to the apple trees and got a piece of sacking full of them. Athel and I made our way down to the village of St Jean. It was a boiling hot day and we had a steep bit of hill to climb before reaching the place where the car was to meet me. When we arrived at the place we sat down by the roadside and ate some apples and chocolate. We waited several hours and the car had not arrived and we were just going to go back to the château when it came rumbling up the hill and took me away back again.

13.9.15 Get up early and arrange my kit and set out for Boulogne at 7am. Arrive there at 8 o'clock and worry about getting passports viséed etc. At 10 o'clock go on to boat and are not long before we are off. Beautifully calm and a very pleasant journey. Arrive at Folkestone and board the train which comes in at Charing Cross in place of Victoria. Then cut across to Victoria and find Sylvia and Viola awaiting me under the clock. As we have some time to wait for the train I deliver a walking stick which I have brought home from Mont Noir for one of Athel's friends and

The view of the site for a military cemetery amid the ruins of Vermelles; a handful of wooden crosses can be seen.

A burial service at Vermelles Military Cemetery, January 1916. The closest grave on the left is that of Private John George Newton of the Hertfordshire Regiment, killed in action on 21 November 1915. The grave on the right closest to the camera is that of Driver James Madden of the Royal Field Artillery, killed in action on 24 November 1915.

also change some five franc notes. Then, off we go to Sutton. At Sutton a cab is waiting and I drive up in state, calling first at Nurse who is staying at Langley Park Rd. Then off we go across the downs at the corner of the lane. We see Elaine who is just coming home from Coveny's and give her a lift in the cab. They are waiting for us outside the gate – Father and Mother.

Go in and have a jolly good tea. In the evening visit cadets parade and find very few on parade but very pleased to see them. Pope and Elliott also drop in and I distribute some French coins and give Pope some fag cards which Athel asked me to deliver. Then go round to see Choat and show some photographs of graves.

14.9.15 At home in morning. Go to Alfred's in the afternoon after visiting the County School and seeing Mr Birks about Rewcastle's grave. Spend the evening at Alfred's and call on nurse on the way home.

15.9.15 Go to London and see all the damage done by Zeppelins. Then call on Kodaks and see J.B. who takes me to lunch at the Holborn. In the evening look in at BLB but there is no parade. See some of the boys and then dismiss them. Walk home with Stapley and Elliott and Pope.

16.9.15 Take family to Hampton Court by river. Start from Westminster bridge. See capture balloon. Have lunch at Hampton Court and then visit the palace and grounds. Everything very pretty and a beautiful day. Return to Sutton by train. In the evening see Rev. Powell and Pascall and decide to suspend BLB. We all cycle round and see Mr Fea.

17.9.15 Go to Brighton with Nurse and see Aunt Polly. AP very much surprised to see us. Have lunch at a very nice restaurant.

Ivan's diary for 1915 ends at this point with the final comment 'see next book'. Unfortunately this hasn't come to light and the next diaries and letters start in January 1917.

On 25 September 1915 the British launched an offensive at Loos (near Lens) which proved disastrous: little gain at enormous cost. It is evident from the photograph collection and brief mention in his memoirs that Ivan was sent repeatedly to this sector from October 1915 until at least January 1916. Athel was also there. There are several photographs from Vermelles where a cemetery was started behind the British lines. Ivan also visited other cemeteries in this sector including the Givenchy (Windy Corner) Guards Cemetery, Cambrin Churchyard and the Cuinchy Royal Berks Cemetery.

> Every now and then I would come across Athel and his field ambulance and would take the opportunity of going to see him: places like Bethune, Dranoutre etc. and I went to Vermelles on the Lens Front where the Prince of Wales chauffeur was killed a few days before. Athel said it was busy work there for ambulance men.

Driver Harry George Green of the Army Service Corps was killed by a German shell hitting the prince's car on 29 September 1915. The prince was busy inspecting troops at the time. Green is buried in Vermelles British Cemetery.

Report of the Work of the GRC

On 21 August 1915 Fabian Ware submitted a 'Report of the work of the GRC' to the Adjutant General at GHQ, which included a section about the Photographic Department:

> Then it was decided by you that we should be exempt from the prohibition to carry cameras and should be allowed to photograph the graves, in response to the demand for photographs from relatives at home, it was decided that, as the places where the graves were situated of which photographs were required were so scattered and various, it was necessary to proceed on a regular system and endeavour to photograph all graves. The Joint War Committee of the British Red Cross Society immediately agreed to provide necessary funds and a Photograph Department was established. The work has developed rapidly. Three first class professional photographers have been employed and have been at work daily in [the] charge of an Officer. They have never hesitated to take photographs as far up towards the firing line as they were permitted to go. We have been utilising the summer months for taking, under favourable conditions, as many negatives as possible so that we shall be in a position to supply prints asked for when the taking of good negatives becomes more difficult. In all, near 2,000 negatives, showing 8,000 graves have been taken and prints are being despatched to relatives as requests come in either from England or from Officers and men serving in France. Over 200 photographs have been despatched and requests have been received for 200 others. The employment of professional photographers has enabled us to send, in most cases excellent though small photographs, and the letters we have received acknowledging them are invariably most appreciative and grateful. In a majority of cases applicants for photographs and recipients of them express a desire to pay any cost which may be incurred. As you are aware, however,

by the generosity of the Joint War Committee of the British Red Cross Society and St John Ambulance the professional photographers and their equipment and material are being supplied free of cost and we are therefore sending out with each photograph a slip bearing the following statement:-

> 'The Joint War Committee of the British Red Cross Society and St John Ambulance, 85 Pall Mall, London, S.W. is at present providing, from subscriptions received, for the expenses of taking these photographs, so that the Graves Registration Commission is able to send them to relatives free of cost.'

In view of the expense incurred by the Joint War Committee in the preparation of these negatives and of the great value which, from the evidence of letters received by us, is attached to them by the relatives of those who have fallen I would submit the question whether it is desirable to allow the Joint War Committee, should they so desire, to make some public announcement of our ability to supply photographs since at present the work of this department is only known to those at home by information supplied from the Front or by persons who have themselves received photographs.

Letters from relatives were not retained in the Commission's archives but there is the odd notable exception. During the Battle of the Somme it became necessary to send photographs to the prime minister himself. Herbert Asquith's son Raymond, a lieutenant in the Grenadier Guards, was killed on 15 September 1916 near Ginchy. He was buried in Guillemont Road Cemetery. Ware received a letter of thanks from David Davies on behalf of Asquith, dated 16 October 1916:

> I have told the Prime Minister of your letter and given him the photographs of Lieutenant Asquith's grave. The Prime Minister asks me to say that he is exceedingly obliged to you for the trouble you have taken in the matter and is very gratified with the arrangements made for his son's burial.

It is very evident that photographs taken by Ivan and his colleagues were much appreciated by relatives and Ware therefore believed that the GRC should be ready to anticipate an ever-increasing flow of requests. The provision of photographs free of cost also meant that no one would be precluded from making such a request.

The photographic work would also increase the need to better maintain the appearance of the cemeteries. Ware noted in his report:

> Sections have been able to call attention to and to rectify various errors and to secure a general improvement in the appearance of cemeteries, a point of some importance since the demand of relatives at home for photographs of graves is steadily increasing. In some instances the GRC has refrained from complying with these requests until the general appearance of the graves has been improved.

By the middle of August 1915 a total of 18,173 graves had been registered by the GRC. The workload would only increase as the initial flow of enquiries turned into a torrent as the work of the Commission became more widely known, not to mention that the two most costly battles of the war for the British army were yet to be fought: the infamous Somme and Passchendaele offensives would each add hundreds of thousands of names to the registers. The work would also need to expand beyond the Western Front to the other theatres of war such as Salonika and the Dardanelles, with each area bringing its own fresh challenges.

Consequently, by October 1915 the Graves Registration Commission was transferred from the British Red Cross to the army, and in February 1916 its name was changed to the Directorate of Graves Registration and Enquiries. The officers of the GRC had held honorary ranks but now they were given commissions and in many cases promoted. Ware was promoted from major to lieutenant colonel and then to brigadier general in August 1916. Lieutenant Wilson was promoted to captain. Ivan had held the rank of orderly while under the Red Cross, and then in April 1916 he was enlisted into the Royal Engineers with the rank of sapper.

The Royal Engineers would have been the designated corps for Ivan since photography had been one of its disciplines since just after the Crimean War. It was the RE who had studied and pioneered the use of photography for military purposes, in particular for reconnaissance.

As a fully-fledged section of the army there was a greater sense of authority in the field for the Graves Registration Units.

A portrait of Ivan in his RE uniform.

Chapter Three

Digs and Darkrooms

Through his writings and photographs Ivan has provided a lot of insight into the various places in which he lived, the equipment he used, and the men who worked alongside him in the Graves Registration Units. It is evident that his accommodation ranged from the rudimentary to the more refined. While he was often billeted in a house or château, his diaries often mention sleeping in unusual places: dugouts, barns, wagons, cellars, on a shelf, out in the open and under canvas. Even in grand châteaux the facilities were often frugal and so the photographers were forced to improvise when it came to developing and printing:

Ivan's colleagues Sergeant T. Comfort, Bert Haddon and Frederick Roper at the improvised darkroom 'Kodak House' in the grounds of Château de Relingue, Lillers, 1915.

> We were to use a 3A (postcard size) FP Kodak on a tripod and stop down to F32 and use a brief time exposure. The whole of the grave was to be included and show background of other graves. The reason for the use of a small aperture like F32 was to get depth of focus and sharpness. We were to use 10 exposure autographic roll film and mark each film with our code letter and number. Bert Haddon was A, I was D, and my first shot was D1. By the end of the war I had reached 28,600.
>
> One of us was to remain at the base to develop and print the work. Developing in a roll film 3½ foot tank, fixing and then washing thoroughly in running water. Afterwards we made contact prints on Velox Paper, washed very thoroughly and toned sepia. Then glazed on glazing sheets. Quite a business.

The camera that Ivan used most often for his work was the No. 3A Folding Pocket Kodak (Model B-4). His original camera survives in excellent condition and full working order and is shown in this photograph. It has a retractable bellows lens and produced 3¼ x 5½ inch postcard format images on Kodak 122 roll film.

The camera has a double release: flexible or pneumatic. The Ball Bearing Shutter allows the time exposure 1/25, 1/50 and 1/100 of a second. The aperture goes from F4 to F128. The camera body was made from wood, covered with leather, and the back and the flap are covered metal; it looks like a high-quality piece of kit. It feels quite lightweight at just over a kilogram. By comparison my Canon 5D Mark II, used for this book, weighs in at a hefty 1.7kg with the kit lens attached.

Roll film was the medium Ivan used most of the time due to its obvious convenience, taking up to 150 exposures in the course of a day's work. He noted on 8 April 1917: 'Average exposures: 400 per week.' However, we know he still used glass plates as all his surviving negatives are in this format. The No. 3A Folding Pocket Kodak could also be used with a glass plate adapter, which Ivan almost certainly possessed. He does mention another camera in his diaries – the '7x5' – which was likely a Kodak that used

Glass plate negative of Lijssenthoek Military Cemetery.

glass plates. Glass plates still remained superior to film in terms of durability and image quality; they were far less likely to bend or distort.

The headquarters of Graves Registration was always near GHQ. First at Lillers, then at Arques near St Omer. Then at Château de Valfosse at Hesdin near Montreuil, and then at villages near St Omer. At each place we had different kinds of places to live. At Lillers we built a shelter of old rubber groundsheets in the Château grounds – Haddon, Roper and I lived in it. It was called Kodak House.

At Arques we lived in bedrooms in the Château itself, a picturesque castle-like house. At Hesdin we lived in rooms in a school building later to move to the Château de Valfosse outside the town, where I and two other fellows lived in a stone summerhouse in the wood.

Later Bert Haddon went permanently to Boulogne and I lived at a farm in a Belgian place called Esquelbecq near Wormhoudt [this was actually in France,

Colleagues of Ivan at Château de Valfosse, Hesdin in 1917.

not Belgium]. Then I moved to Poperinghe and later on I was stationed at Ypres in a dug-out near the Cavalry Barracks, and finally at Brielen (Ypres) in a château, [the Trois Tours Château] and later to a POW camp at Brielen.

At each of these places it was necessary to rig up darkrooms and washing arrangements. At Lillers the darkroom and printing room was a cellar in the château. For washing we had a big tank of water filled by buckets from a spray. The films were attached to laths of wood placed in a long box and the water from the tank ran into this by a rubber hose.

At Arques we occupied a summerhouse near the river side using this as a darkroom and printing room. First of all we tried washing the films in the river itself until we discovered it fed a water mill and the water sank to a trickle every now and then. So after that we had our big tanks and filled it from the river with buckets. To fill the buckets we had a plank like a diving board fixed to the bank. One day we found it had been sabotaged but we noticed it in time before falling in to the river.

At Hesdin we had a proper portable darkroom made and as there was running water at this school were able to wash films in the kitchen. At Valfosse Château we filled our water tank again from a pump supplied by a horse walking round a mechanical device but used so much water that the horse pump broke down and the Royal Engineers installed a chain pump run by a little petrol motor.

Ivan (left) and Haddon washing films by the river at Arques in the snow.

This was alright until we had such a severe winter in 1917 that the temperature dropped to about 22° F. Films froze as they came out of the washing tank. This put a stop to processing on the field and Haddon went to Boulogne to set up a proper D & P [Developing and Printing] department. Henceforth us photographers were always at Sections taking photos of graves.

A postcard photograph of Bert Haddon sent to Ivan at Christmas in 1917. Haddon gets the most mention out of Ivan's colleagues in the diaries and was likely his closest pal from the war.

Ivan and Haddon having a snowball fight with Roper outside the summerhouse darkroom in Arques, winter 1915–16.

Ivan pretending to cut Roper's hair, winter 1915–16.

On this postcard from Hesdin, dated 8 June 1916, Ivan wrote to his mother: 'This PC shows the playground and the windows opposite our darkroom (which is the opposite side of the corridor). Needless to say the news of K's death came as a great blow to everyone [Lord Kitchener had perished aboard the HMS *Hampshire* when she struck a mine on 5 June 1916]. The King's message was sent around this afternoon. No fresh news yet.'

The Château de Valfosse, Hesdin. The huts on the right were the photographic darkrooms. The GRC photographers moved here in October 1916.

Graves Registration Unit personnel at Esquelbecq, 1918.

Lillers, Arques and Hesdin are in the Pas-de-Calais region of northern France. This sector was well behind the front line for most of the war until the Germans advanced in April 1918, capturing towns such as Bailleul. The advance was halted just shy of Hazebrouck and Béthune. Therefore, for much of the war, Ivan was able to move around this region of France relatively freely, although some areas were vulnerable to air-raids.

In April 1918 the French village of Esquelbecq became a base of operation for two casualty clearing stations and Ivan's GR Unit as the German advance necessitated a hasty withdrawal. The GRUs were based on a farm. The village lies halfway between Dunkirk and Hazebrouck, and about 8 miles west of the Belgian border.

Graves Registration Unit personnel at Esquelbecq, 1918.

Ivan noted on the back of this photograph: 'My old billet in the lock up at the Cavalry Barracks [at Ypres]. The sunken stream Yperlee runs in between camera and billet.' The covered doorway on the left was 'the home of the motorbike' and the small opening 'my bedroom window'. He was based here from April 1919.

On the moat at Ypres in 1919. Lack of adequate darkroom facilities would often force Ivan and his colleagues to use improvised means to carry out their photographic work. In this picture a home-made raft is being used to tow films and prints on a wooden frame in order to wash them.

Photography during the First World War

Early photography was largely a professional pursuit but as the Victorian age drew to an end it was increasingly accessible to the masses. In 1889 Kodak introduced the first commercial transparent roll film that would eventually supersede the use of glass plates, and then in 1898 the first Folding Pocket Kodak came on the market. This meant that by the early 1900s taking photographs was greatly simplified and no longer just the domain of the professional. In spite of a general army ban on photography, many British soldiers took cameras – in particular the very popular Vest Pocket Kodak (VPK) – with them to war in 1914. Some Kodak advertisements aimed the VPK directly at soldiers:

> Snapshots of the war – pictures that will later on be of immense value – can be taken if you put a Vest Pocket Kodak in your kit. The Autographic-Kodak is exactly suited to the soldier's requirements – it is 'the Soldier's Kodak.' Light in weight, it is easy to carry; small, therefore takes up little room; very strong, exposed parts are rustproof and will stand hard usage.

At first the restrictions were somewhat lax and what a soldier could get away with depended on the strictness of his immediate superiors. The famed Christmas Truce of 1914 especially highlights that this ban was frequently being ignored. Numerous photos of fraternization were taken and made it on to the front page of British newspapers. Such photos infuriated the military top brass as they fuelled press sensationalism and went against the tone of anti-German propaganda, showing Tommy and Fritz together in their common humanity. These were not considered ideal sentiments for prosecuting a war.

More generally speaking, there were two major concerns about photography: firstly, to restrict what the Press might share with the British public about the realities of life at the front; and secondly the security risk of leaking intelligence to the enemy. Newspaper demand for photos increased, offering significant sums of money, as did the potential punishment for unauthorized use of cameras at the front. The army chiefs clamped down by issuing a War Office Instruction on 16 March 1915 declaring a total ban on the possession of any photographic equipment by officers and other ranks alike. Unauthorized possession of a camera was now a court-martial offence. Punishment included imprisonment and hard labour.

The VPK was produced between 1912 and 1926. Ivan owned the autographic version that was produced from 1915, shown in this photograph. It is not in as good condition as his FPK but is in working order. The camera has a single achromatic lens located behind the shutter. The aperture has four settings related to distance and brightness and the shutter can be set to 1/25, 1/50 or 'Bulb' and 'Time'. It took Autographic A-127 film and has a small trapdoor at the back that allows the photographer to write on the film with a metal stylus between each negative. The VPK at 250g is a quarter of the weight of the FPK and measures 12 x 6.2 x 2.5cm. Ivan mentions his VPK only once in his diaries and it was probably little used by him as the FPK would have produced sharper images. However, it was no doubt a useful back-up camera.

After this point there was a sharp decline in casual shots from the trenches taken by British and Commonwealth servicemen since most, though not all, complied with this regulation. Photography at the front would largely be left to a small number of official photographers. This meant that strict regulations regarding the use of cameras were in place by the time the GRC decided it was necessary to initiate a photographic department in May 1915. Lieutenant Wilson noted in his draft scheme of 21 May:

> Any scheme of organisation for doing such work must conform with the directions of the A.G. contained in his Memorandum of 3rd April 1915 but, in my opinion, the regulation under paragraph 3, of that memorandum, Vis., that the camera shall be sealed before being taken out and be returned to the proper Officer to have the seal broken and the film removed, is unworkable as in the ordinary course of a day's photography work of this character several films will be used and arrangements can easily be made to ensure that a strict account is given of all films issued without resorting to inconvenience of sealing up the camera. I will therefore assume that the necessary alteration will be made in this regulation.

The GRC then finalized 'Instructions for Photographers in the Field' that highlighted the control to be exerted over photographic equipment:

> All photographic material is to be obtained direct from the officer in charge of Photographic Department, H.Q. GRC. Each reel of film issued to photographer must be returned to Photo Dept., whether used or unused, or spoilt. No person engaged in photographic work carried on by the GRC shall have in his possession any camera or photographic material of any kind, and persons engaged in such work are warned that the mere fact of being found in possession of any photographic material, save such as is carried by the authority of the OC GRC, commits a grave military offence. Any such camera or photographic material found on such person will be immediately confiscated, and not only will such person be dismissed [from] the service of the GRC, but he will also be reported to the Provost Marshall [*sic*], and be dealt with under military law.
>
> Each person engaged in such photographic work shall only take such photographs as he receives definite orders to take.

Ivan's work was therefore, at least initially, heavily supervised and certainly his diary entries in 1915 show that he was usually accompanied by an officer such as Lieutenant (later Captain) Wilson. He would also have to carry authority papers, not only to access certain areas along the front but also to be able to carry a camera. He couldn't take pictures of whatever he pleased until freedom of photography was declared shortly after the armistice. He noted in his memoirs:

> About the quietest sector was Armentières and here a man called Sgt. Callow took me to some of the very advanced cemeteries close to the front line. On one occasion I went with an officer called Capt. Fraser to a cemetery reached by a communication trench and we were arrested because I was carrying a camera. We were marched back under escort by armed men to the HQ where after exhibiting our credentials we were at liberty again.

Ivan's papers include a document titled 'Photography' produced by the Graves Registration HQ that provided photographers with some clear regulations to follow. Here are some excerpts:

1. Where a photographer for any reason takes a photograph of a grave which is not in good order he shall on his exposure note explain the local conditions answerable

An example of one of Ivan's authority passes, signed by Captain Charles Wilson.

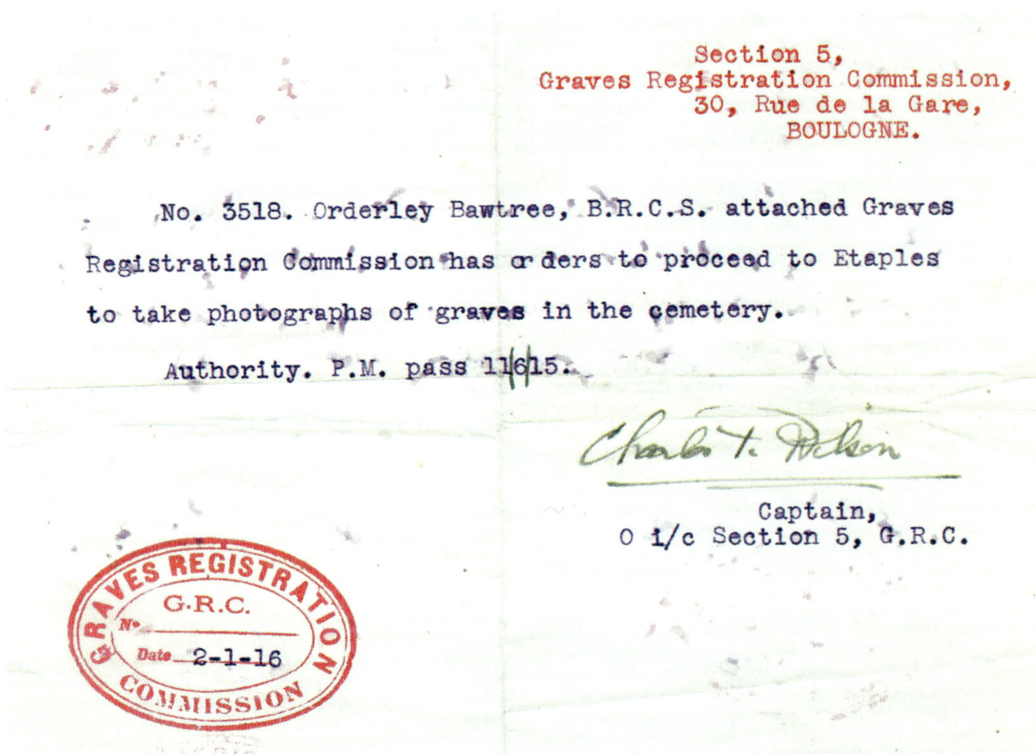

Section 5,
Graves Registration Commission,
30, Rue de la Gare,
BOULOGNE.

No. 3518. Orderley Bawtree, B.R.C.S. attached Graves Registration Commission has orders to proceed to Etaples to take photographs of graves in the cemetery.

Authority. P.M. pass 11/6/15.

Captain,
O i/c Section 5, G.R.C.

GRAVES REGISTRATION COMMISSION
G.R.C.
No.
Date 2-1-16

for the state of the grave, as for example, that it was taken on a battlefield, or in an advanced divisional cemetery, or other reasons and shall submit this to the O.i/c., of the section in which he is working, who shall, (if desirable), further submit it to the O.C. the Unit. This exposure note shall be sent, together with the other exposure notes, with the films to be developed to H.Q., G.R. Units together with the notes or comments which the Officer in charge of the section or the O.C. the Unit may see fit to add in explanation.

2. There shall be kept by each Unit a photography book for each cemetery or group of cemeteries in the Unit area, in the form decided on by the O.C., G.R. Units. In these books the photographers shall enter up alphabetically under cemetery headings the lists of requests received from Headquarters, and the books must at all times be kept up to date.
3. That there may be as much uniformity as possible in the photographic work.
4. In view of the increasing number of applications for photographs which are being received, it is of the greatest importance that the output of negatives shall be as high as possible consistent with good work, and no opportunity should be neglected of which the conditions of light, the exigencies of transport, and the military situation will permit.

By 1917, 12,000 photographs had been dispatched to relatives and by March that year it had become apparent that three photographers would no longer be enough to keep up with the increasing backlog of work. On 27 April Ivan noted '760 photo requests for Section C to date' and he repeatedly wrote in his diary 'lot of new requests arrive'. Ware noted that 'the question of photographers has become more urgent' and 'that it will be necessary... immediately to put forward the proposal that seven of the clerks on our present establishment should be transferred to RE photographers.' Ivan mentioned the arrival of a new photographer, Private Cobb, to his unit on 13 May.

Report of the Photographic Work of the Directorate

A report written on 28 June 1918 by Lieutenant Colonel G.H. Stobart, AAG, provides an excellent summary of the photographic work. Here is an abridged version:

> Shortly after the formation of the Graves Registration Commission in 1915, suggestions were made that the photographing of graves and despatching of prints to relatives would meet a public need, more especially in those cases where, owing to distance, expense, or other causes, it would be impossible for relatives to carry out their desire of visiting graves after the War. As a result the foundation

was laid of the present system of supplying photographs of individual graves, the first being taken in May 1915.

The photographic staff for some considerable time consisted only of 3 photographers, who, in addition to taking the photographs, managed the developing and printing up to the time that part of the Directorate office (including the despatching and records portion of the photographic branch) was transferred to the War Office in August 1916.

From that date until 18th May 1918, 85,000 requests for photographs have been noted in the Department, and 51,300 negatives have been received from France. As many negatives include more than one grave, the number of requests complied with is considerably in excess of this total, and the total number of graves photographed is 66,423. This latter number, however, does not include all the photographs which have been taken in France since February 1918. A number of these have been held up and not yet printed owing to the military situation.

In August 1917, it was found necessary to suspend the photographing of graves in the area of the Somme Battlefields owing to the lack of transport and the time taken in locating isolated graves. Previous to this a small number of isolated graves had been photographed in this area.

The original procedure was for the photographs to be taken and developed in France by DGR&E, and forwarded to London for printing. In July 1917, this procedure was discontinued, and the negatives were developed and prints made by Army Printing and Stationery Services, France, with the result that we have received better prints and there has been a considerable saving in expense.

Since the middle of April 1918, it has been found necessary to suspend practically all photography except in Base and Lines of Communication Cemeteries. A small number of requests, however, have been sent out for various other cemeteries, in case it was found possible to resume operations.

All the negatives are systematically numbered and filed in this office, so that should any further request be received for a photograph of a grave, a fresh print can be provided.

It may safely be stated that no portion of the work of the Directorate has given greater comfort and satisfaction to the general public than the provision of these photographs.

Although the photographers have been supplied by the Army, the whole cost of the cameras, films, paper, chemicals and printing and developing apparatus, together with part of the expenses of transport has been defrayed by the Joint War Committee of the British Red Cross Society.

Chapter Four

Shellfire and Shrapnel

Initially when Ivan arrived in France in June 1915 he did not see much of the 'business of war'. In fact, he seemed more concerned about his family in London who were facing the threat of Zeppelin air-raids. The first raid on London was on 31 May 1915. Subsequent raids are documented by his sister Viola who no doubt wrote to him about it. He wrote the following in two letters to Viola from his first month in France:

A lorry makes its way down the shell-damaged Rue de Lille, Bailleul.

> It strikes me that I shall spend a lot of my time developing etc as things go at present. It is funny that nearly everyone except me has seen something of the business even if it is only planes being shelled. The latter, by the by is a very dangerous pastime if they are anywhere near, for it is a clear law of nature that whatever goes up must come down sooner or later. I saw a picture of French soldiers wearing steel caps to protect them from such aerial missiles.
>
> I expect I shall soon see the same sight as Athel for I hear that aeroplanes can be seen with shrapnel round them nearly every evening at the top of the ridge near our Château. They tell me that it is a wonderful sight.
>
> I am sorry for you poor people in England. It must be very dangerous now that all these Zeppelins are about. I have not seen a Taube [a German aeroplane] yet. A great many English aeroplanes pass over daily.

In a letter to an unknown recipient (probably to one of the sisters), Athel provides a curious insight into the French soldier's (Poilu's) mentality for coping with bombs and shells:

> I must give you an idea of the Poilu's philosophy, as described to me by the CO. This is not it exactly, but gives you the idea. The Poilu says – 'If there is a moonlight night it might not be fine enough for hostile aircraft. If it is, he may not take advantage of it. If he does he may not choose to visit my district. If he does, he may not come to my part of it. If he does, the bombs may not be near me. If one does fall near me, I may not get hit. If I do I may not be seriously hurt. If I am, I may recover. If I don't, or if I am killed altogether – "ce ne fait rien, c'est fini." It will not trouble me, for I shall not know.' How do you like that for philosophy? No time to write more.

Ivan's boss Jim Brown from Kodak wrote to him in June 1915 advising the following: 'Keep well out of the way of shells, bullets, and all lethal weapons as it would never do for an official recorder of bone orchards to be himself planted.'

The apparently cushy start for Ivan's work would certainly change. While he was not fighting in the front line, it is clear that he was often in close proximity to it. Shelling was a continual hazard throughout the war and was the greatest cause of casualties. German long-range guns and aerial attacks also meant both servicemen and civilians could be under fire much further behind the lines. The infamous German howitzer 'Big Bertha', for example, had a range of 9 miles, while the biggest gun of all, the 'Paris

Gun', had an incredible range of 75 miles. When Paris was hit by shells people thought it must have been a Zeppelin attack.

The Graves Registration Units were therefore by no means immune to hostile fire. Fabian Ware addressed the question of danger in his report dated 21 August 1915:

> Owing to the willing assistance that has been given to our Officers by all formations at the front it has been possible for them to do an amount of invaluable work in marking and identifying graves far nearer the firing line than was originally intended. I have issued very strict instructions to all the Sections as to incurring risks, but Officers have strongly represented to me that the very best moral impression is created among the men who are constantly engaged in fighting by seeing that the graves of those who had fallen were being properly looked after, and therefore, in one or two cases, where an officer has desired to work in districts that theoretically were dangerous I have not felt justified in too strictly enforcing the prohibition. So far, thanks to the advice which has been given by various formations and owing to the experience which our Officers are gaining, there have been no actual casualties among members of the GRC. After all, it is difficult to see that in their daily work near the front they run greater risks than in living in towns which are not infrequently shelled, and I would therefore submit that the present arrangement should be allowed to continue if for no better reason, because it is impossible to lay down any hard and fast rule which shall ensure the work being carried on on the principle that no risks are to be run.

In a GRC report regarding the Béthune Section it is highlighted that the work of graves registration could not be adequately carried out without risk:

> One of the chief difficulties of the GRC Section Commander is the necessity of getting to the graves at the earliest possible moment, that is before the marks of identification can become obliterated. This involves frequently working under fire but, in my opinion, is essential to avoid losing the identities and should be left entirely at the discretion of the Officer in charge of the Section.

Ivan makes numerous references in his diaries and letters to the din of the guns and frequent hazards of enemy shellfire. Often he had to dodge shrapnel, run for cover or change routes. On one occasion his camera stand got hit. His billet also got hit on various occasions, compelling him to take refuge in the cellar. In spite of these perils, casualties among those working with the Graves Registration Units were almost nonexistent, which is statistically remarkable. While several men were wounded the only fatality I have been able to find was that of Captain John Doran MacDonald who was wounded by shellfire while erecting crosses on the Menin Road. He died of his wounds on 18 March 1916 and is buried in Bailleul Communal Cemetery Extension. According to Corporal Reginald Bryan, a clerk in the GRC (who was based in Lillers and Arques when Ivan was there), Captain MacDonald was not averse to taking risks:

> The officer in charge of our Section was Captain MacDonald, a very nice gentleman, but rather too risky in going up the line – eventually, early in 1916, he was killed by a stray piece of shrapnel whilst he was watching a bombardment on the Ypres-Menin Road. On many occasions he would go into the front line trenches in order to put a cross on a grave or to see a chaplain and he had many escapes in his car from shells and snipers but, unfortunately, he paid the penalty in the end. On the occasion of his burial, in the very cemetery within five minutes walk of the Bailleul office, a large number of our officers and men attended and full military honours were carried out.

Bryan recounted his first experience of being under fire while visiting cemeteries around Ploegsteert Wood on 26 August 1915:

> We could hear the guns going off and could see the smoke of the shells bursting in the wood – we turned off at the church to the left down a long, straight road, with tall trees on both sides. Evidently their observation balloons must have sighted the car as two or three shells came over in front of us. As we wanted to go on to a place named 'Hyde Park Corner' my officer decided to go on but when we arrived we found it was becoming very 'hot'. We could hear the shells bursting somewhere in the wood, and a Staff Officer told us we had better clear out while we were safe. As shells were bursting on the road we had just come, we simply had to make a dash through the wood. The old motorcar went along like a thing alive and all the time we could hear the 'boom' of the shells and that shrilly whistle. When the Tommies heard a shell they all dashed into their dug-outs or behind shelter and even then it struck me as being rather comical to see them skelter like a lot of rabbits – but evidently they knew more of the danger of shrapnel than I did! After several minutes of scorching however, we managed to clear the wood and get into comparative safety.

Cemeteries near the front were often under fire, making the work of caring for graves all the more 'exciting' as Bryan noted when he visited the northernmost sector in Belgium:

> On one occasion I went up to the front to some of the forward cemeteries at Coxyde, Adinkerke and La Panne. The men in some of these cemeteries had some exciting experiences owing to their proximity to the line. Several times shells dropped into the cemetery where they were working and exploded, but they all escaped injury.

Ivan recounted a few brief anecdotes of incidents where enemy attention got a bit close for comfort. It would seem that he also was at times not averse to a bit of danger:

> One day in a cemetery at Voormezeele [on the south side of Ypres, probably 21/10/17 according to Ivan's diary] I was taking a picture just in front of a Naval 6-inch gun and was so busy I did not realise they were going to fire. As they fired, I and the camera bounced in the air. If shelling got too heavy the officer would withdraw us. One day he very nearly got hit and was bowled over while we hid behind a tree to dodge the shell splinters.
>
> Another time at Dickebusch [to the south-west of Ypres] I and the officer stood talking at his dug-out entrance. He said quite casually, 'I think it would be a good idea to move from here as Jerry has his balloons up and may think we would be a suitable target.' We just started to move off when we heard the thud of one of his long-range guns and the whizz of a shell approaching. We threw ourselves down and got a shower of earth and things all over us but nobody was hurt. Where we had been standing at the dug-out entrance was a big shell-hole. It made us think that did.
>
> There was a big lake at Dickebusch, half water and half mud and reeds and rushes. A duckboard track led right across it and this was the way we went when we wanted to go to Ridgewood Cemetery. Another remembrance of Dickebusch was a period of deep snow when no work could be done. And we lived cosily in a dug-out with a stove in it and read books and played cards. I learnt to play whist there.
>
> Yet another incident was when a NZ concert party put on a show in a huge marquee near the village. They presented *Chu Chin Chow* [this was a musical comedy, based upon *Ali Baba and the Forty Thieves*, which was a big hit in London from 1916]. Quite a wonderful performance under such conditions within hearing of the line, distant machine-gun fire and gunfire.
>
> Kemmel was a place often visited when the cemetery was close to a howitzer battery of 9.2 [inch] guns making an awe inspiring din and attracting enemy attention from time to time. Being near a battery, enemy aircraft often went over

observing and we were ordered to stand perfectly still when a warning whistle sounded and never to look up until the all clear whistle calls sounded.

Some of the cemeteries round Ypres were pretty lively such as Railway Dugouts and Spoilbank near Hill 60 and Essex Farm, Boesinghe. I had a special photo request for that cemetery one day and the officer I was with said it was too lively for photography.

However, not wishing to fail I went by myself and took the photo. I rather think that this incident and others like it resulted in me being mentioned in dispatches [Ivan is listed in Sir Douglas Haig's dispatch in the *London Gazette* on Friday, 14 December 1917; see appendix].

Things got more and more lively as time went on.

A typical bit of Railway Dugouts Burial Ground after a strafe, showing the grave of Gunner Walter Wills of the Canadian Field Artillery, killed in action on 16 June 1916. Note the fallen cross in a waterlogged shell hole.

Ivan's 1917 diary provides further insight into the military activity around him and the hazards he faced:

28.2.17 Go to Vlamertinghe, take photos in cemetery and Hop Store. Lots of dud shells come over. Go to Hospital Farm, Ferme Olivier and then to prison. Take photos in cemeteries. Wait for officer. Then return to Bailleul and clerical work till 8 o'clock. Evening as usual. Hot bath.

9.3.17 Cold snowy weather. Go to Kemmel but do not work at Château as working party and shrapnel. Work at La Clytte and Reninghelst. Belgian boy run over by lorry. Office work in afternoon. Evening as usual.

11.3.17 Go to Ypres Prison and then walk through Cathedral and Menin Gate to Potijze. See air fight and two British machines brought down, aviator falls separate. Work in large cemetery, kitchen garden and Château Lawn. Then walk back and take odd grave in field to left of road. Plenty of shrapnel all the way back. A bit glances off Cpl. Rye's back. Work in prison and return to Bailleul. Go to service at Y.M.C.A. in evening.

15.3.17 Go to Ypres Prison and walk to La Brique. Dodge lyddite [a form of high explosive] at ramparts. From La Brique walk to St Jean White House. Take 80. Plenty of German shelling near Prison. Make a detour to get back safely and return via Sally Port. Make a dash out of prison, during interval Cpl. Rye returns with file. Clerical work in afternoon. Chess etc. in evening.

17.3.17 Fine spring weather. Go with Cpl. Day to Kemmel. Plenty of aeroplanes up and a little shelling but it gets quiet. Walk to Laiterie and then to Lindenhoek Chalet. Have café and biscuits at French shop in town. Go to R.E. Farm and return by Locre and Dranoutre, 80 exposures. Clerical work in afternoon. Evening as usual.

21.3.17 Write to Joan [niece]. Cold snowy morning. Go to Essex Farm and work on Bard Cottage, Marengo and Essex cemetery. Take 64. Return with Cpl. Pool to car. Plenty of big shells on battery to left of road all the morning. Bit catches camera stand and dents on way back. Clerical work in afternoon and evening.

24.3.17 Fine day. Go in box car to Cité Bon Jean via Laventie, Fleurbaix. Road shelled, try alternative and that also shelled. Go by third route OK. Take 130 in Cité Bon Jean. Work late in evening.

1.4.17 Go to Fleurbaix and walk with Cpl. Cotman to Croix Blanche. Big bangs at side of cemetery. Walk on to Rue de Bois. Return to Fleurbaix via Croix Blanche and the churchyard. Take 50. Go to service at Y.M.C.A. in evening. Parcel from nurse.

5.4.17 Cycle to Cité Bon Jean and then with Sgt. Callow to Chapelle d'Armentières, visit all cemeteries. Trench to Ferme Biez under watch, scramble out and keep low. Work in Cité Bon Jean, Erquinghem and Sailly.

6.4.17 Cycle to Cité Bon Jean (road from Erquinghem shelled). Cycle with Sgt. Callow to Houplines, L'Epeneth Road, Ferme Buterne, Aire and New Military, then to Ferme Philippeaux and odd grave, then Old Military. Watch our trenches being bombarded. Ride through Houplines and back to Estaires. Work in cemetery. Office work late.

13.4.17 Car to Pont de Nieppe. Walk to LRB [London Rifle Brigade], Gunners Farm then shell arrives up flooded trench to Tancrez Farm. Return via Le Bizet convent to Pont de Nieppe. Dry feet and return to Estaires. Clerical work late.

14.4.17 Go to Neuve Eglise by box-car. Then walk to Wulverghem. Take one opposite church, then walk in St Quentin's Cabaret. See ammunition dump blown up. Return via Cité Bon Jean and Sailly. Clerical work. Go to Bailleul in the evening.

19.4.17 Go to Hesdin 7.30 am. Steering gear breaks. See lots of tanks. Have talk with Haddon etc. See André in the town. See moving tank on way back. Work late in office.

22.4.17 Cycle to Lijssenthoek and Poperinghe. Take 75. Go to Y.M.C.A. service as usual. Bomb dropped at dinner time. Work in office, dinner etc. as usual. Receive parcel from Inksters.

28.4.17 Go in car to Kruikstraate [*sic*, probably Kruisstraat] and walk to Railway Dugouts. Take 110 photos and walk back to car via Shrapnel Corner. See plenty of preparations for offensive. Office work in afternoon. Letters etc. in evening.

30.4.17 Go to Bedford House – everything torn up by bombardment. Take 15 photos and return with men and kits. Have to go via Shrapnel Corner on account of severe shelling. Afternoon in office. Pictures in evening.

4.5.17 Work in office in morning. In afternoon go to Erquinghem, Pont de Nieppe, Romarin and Steenwerck. See a lot of batteries which the Germans have knocked out. In evening sit in garden of farm. 4 bombs at 10 o'clock.

Bedford House Cemetery, Ypres. The grave of Gunner Francis Provis of the Australian Field Artillery appears to have suffered a direct hit from a shell. The original cross is lying in pieces either side of a large shell hole and has been replaced. This highlights the importance of accurate and hasty registration of graves as cemeteries such as Bedford House were often prone to shelling. Provis had died from shrapnel wounds in his back on 9 October 1916, aged 19. His AIF cap badge has been attached to the top of the cross.

23.5.17 Go to Essex Farm, Marengo Farm and Bard Cottage. Plenty of aerial activity. Lots of traffic and big guns about. Bailleul in afternoon. Cobb goes to Lijssenthoek etc. and Mendinghem. Tenu Pas in evening. 9d. beer.

24.5.17 Go for joy-ride to Mont-des-Cats and tidy up the cemeteries. In afternoon go to Kemmel and take 10 photos. Great activity everywhere. Tenu Pas in evening (3 glasses).

31.5.17 Absolutely nothing doing. Lounge about all day. See one of our balloons brought down in flames. 2 beers.

22.7.17 Have easy day. Cycle to Watou, La Eng and get bath. Enter up new requests in afternoon. Go to service at Watou in evening. Loud air raids at night.

24.7.17 In morning go to Essex Farm. Cemetery in terrible state. Air foul and tear gas about. Return via Vlamertinghe, Ferme Olivier and Brandhoek. In afternoon try to visit Bard Cottage but strafe on. Visit Mendinghem and then make notes up. Sleep out in open.

Essex Farm Military Cemetery, Boesinghe, on the north side of Ypres. This cemetery has visibly suffered from shellfire with splintered trees lining the canal bank and debris littering the foreground.

25.7.17 Very wet in morning. In afternoon cycle to Bard Cottage. Take four photos. Strafe on. Have tea at Vlamertinghe. Pack up in the evening. Sleep out all night.

27.7.17 Move in car to Bailleul in morning and see all the boys. Have afternoon off. Fritz bangs away at town every two hours. Dinner in the evening and then elope to farm and spend night in open.

2.8.17 Go to Voormezeele in car and walk to St Eloi. Too much doing at Chester Farm to get there. Go to Oak Dump but have to clear out. Go to Damme Strasse and return via Bus House. In afternoon see Jack [Ivan's cousin Jack Lilley]. In evening go over on bike to Estaires.

4.8.17 Go in car to Vierstraat and walk to Kleine Vierstraat, Ferme Godezonne and Rest-and-be-thankful Farm. Then on to Kemmel. Swift shells into Kemmel. Return in car. New requests in afternoon. Sleep at billet.

5.8.17 Weather clears up. Go in car to Voormezeele and walk to Bus House. Take photos and walk to Chester Farm and Spoilbank. Return via La Laiterie and Kemmel. In afternoon go to Dranoutre, Kemmel, Irish House, La Clytte and Locre. Go to service at Y.M.C.A. Germans do a bit more damage to Rue de Lille. Sleep out.

6.8.17 Car to Voormezeele and walk to Shelly Farm. Get shelled out. Walk to Damme Strasse and Pheasant Wood and explore Ravine Wood. Get shelled out and Mr. Day got slightly wounded. Make off for Voormezeele. Leave camera stand behind.

13.8.17 Try and get to Le Bizet but roads under fire. Go to Wulverghem instead. In afternoon go to Plus Douve Farm and take one photo. Very lively.

22.8.17 Car to Ypres. Strafe on. Work in Menin-Road-South Cemetery but soon have to come away on account of shrapnel. Take odd grave in Vlamertinghe. Go to Mendinghem in afternoon. See aeroplane brought down at night. 180 new requests arrive.

A distant view of Kemmel beyond the ruins on the south-east side of Ypres, from Menin Road South Cemetery.

4.9.17 Car to Kruisstraat and walk to Lille-Gate. Too lively to reach Menin Road. Walk across to Railway Dugouts. Have to come away in a hurry. Return via Shrapnel Corner and Vlamertinghe. Ford car gets bombed in afternoon. Sleep in cellar.

15.9.17 Work in office all day. Shell lands close to office. New photo lists arrive. Sleep in cellar.

19.9.17 Car to Kemmel, Irish House, Lindenhoek Chalet, Packhorse Farm, Pond Farm, St Quentin's Cabaret, Westhoff Farm. Work in Bailleul in afternoon. Many shells on Bailleul.

20.9.17 6am: new advance starts with success. Car to Voormezeele. See bombardment, balloons, aeroplanes by the thousand. Long line of British and German wounded, German prisoners. Work at Elzenwalle Château and Brewery, Ridgewood, Kleine Vierstraat and Rest-and-be-thankful Farm. Evening as usual.

15.10.17 Car to Voormezeele and Locre 8 and Bedford House. Can't get through Ypres on account of shelling. Go to Belgian Battery Corner and Château Belge. Office work in afternoon. Evening as usual.

21.10.17 Car to Voormezeele. Walk to Spoilbank and Bus House and work in Voormezeele. Big guns firing. Office in afternoon. Service at Caisse D'Epargne in evening.

28.10.17 Car to Vlamertinghe. Rather wet morning. Big battle going on. Stapley comes in afternoon. Tea at billet. Service at Caisse D'Epargne in evening.

29.10.17 Cycle to La Clytte and Dickebusch. See aeroplanes practising firing on roads. Work in Bailleul. Evening as usual.

30.10.17 Dull weather. Shells all day long. E.F.C. gets hit. Cycle to Dranoutre and Kemmel district, Gordon Cemetery and old trenches. Lot of new requests arrive.

5.12.17 Father birthday 71. Car to Voormezeele (a bit lively), Dickebusch and The Huts. See Jack going up on to lorry. Clerical work. Lijssenthoek sheled.

The Battle of Messines, June 1917

This is the British offensive that receives the biggest mention in Ivan's material, probably because the shockwaves of the initial attack were felt as far away as London and he was only 7 miles away. This offensive began, as usual, with a massive artillery bombardment, but is largely remembered for the series of enormous underground mines that were detonated – nineteen in total – and devastated the German front line. The mines went off along the Messines Ridge, which stretched from Hill 60 just outside Ypres down to Ploegsteert close to the border with France, at 3.10 am on 7 June 1917. The offensive was deemed a great success in removing the Germans from this much-coveted high ground of the Ypres Salient and was a prelude to the Passchendaele offensive that began on 31 July 1917.

> I used to like living at the Bailleul Section and was there on the night the Messines mine was exploded. The whole of our billet swayed about and then the front came to life with Very lights [flares] and artillery and aeroplanes. Up to that time Bailleul had not been under shell fire, but from then on it received quite a lot of enemy attention both day and night.

Ivan recorded the following in his diary:

> **1.6.17** Go to Lijssenthoek, La Clytte and Dranoutre. See house on fire near Lijssenthoek. See ammo dump go up at La Clytte. Hang about in afternoon. See one of our aeroplanes catch fire and pilot burnt to death. Evening as usual. 2 beers.

> **3.6.17** Go to Lijssenthoek, Reninghelst and then Dickebusch. Very lively. Take no photos. See big bombardment of Wytschaete. Brig. Gen. Ware and Capt. Taylor arrive. Bailleul shelled. Go to Capt. Taylor. Go to service at Caisse D'Epargne. See some triplanes.

The remains of Wytschaete, a village very close to Messines, which was taken by the British during the advance of June 1917.

4.6.17 Go to Locre, La Clytte, Ouderdom, Vlamertinghe, Poperinghe and back over Mt. Noir. In afternoon go to Estaires. Take photos of wounded man at Trois Arbres.

5.6.17 Ammunition train blows up in morning. Go to Lijssenthoek, Poperinghe, Mendinghem and Houtekirk. In afternoon go for a walk.

6.6.17 Go to Boulogne via Hazebrouck, Arques, Lumbres. See Athel. Collect pegs. Go for walk and to tea with Athel. Return in thunder storm and get soaked. Big bombardment during the night.

The below photograph is of one of the huge mine craters on the Messines Ridge. A man can be seen bending down in the snow on the far bank of the crater. It is most likely the Spanbroekmolen crater, which was created by an explosive charge of 91,000lb of ammonal. It is the largest of the mine craters from the Battle of Messines.

The Spanbroekmolen mine crater in 2015, which came to be known as the Pool of Peace.

> **7.6.17** Great Messines Battle. 3.10am get shaken all over the place by the mines exploding. Then terrific bombardment for an hour. See S.O.S. signals and Very lights. Wounded passing down street all the morning. Rue de Lille shelled. In afternoon go back to H.Q. via Merville and Bethune. Get caught in storm. See Haddon.

> **7.9.17** Go to Westhoff Farm, Kandahar Farm and then search for graves in old front-line near R.E. Farm. See Messines and Wytschaete and huge mine craters. Take photos at Kemmel. Bombs on flying ground on way back. Have hot bath in afternoon.

Ivan writes much more about what was going on around the time of the Battle of Messines in this letter to his mother dated 10 June 1917:

> We have all been very unsettled lately, owing to expecting that big push at any moment. Preparations had been going on for months, though of course I mentioned nothing of it in my letters. Guns of all kinds were rumbling day and night down our street, aeroplanes always on the move, umpteen sausages up everywhere observing, and big collections of ammunition; lorries, buses and all

kinds of traffic filling up the roads so that it was difficult to get along. Rumours kept on floating about that it was to be tomorrow – or the next day – or in a week – or in a month, but nobody quite knew when. We heard also of the big mines that were all ready to go up. In addition to activity of this description, the enemy's artillery was very active all along our district, and it was impossible to get to a number of cemeteries. The result was that I began to run out of work. All these factors contributed to the poor attempts at letters that I made.

On June 1st I went round to various cemeteries. Whilst working in one I saw an ammunition dump blown up. It went up with a mighty thump, and sent a cloud of smoke into the air a mile high. The same evening one of our machines had a mishap just in the field behind the billet, and burst into flames. All efforts to put it out were unavailing, and the poor chap inside was burnt to a cinder. It was his trial flight.

On June 2nd nothing particular happened but the Germans had a shot or two at our railway station which lies some distance from the town. This put the wind up many of the civilians, a few of whom packed up their belongings and cleared.

On the 3rd I visited a town quite close to where the advance has been made, thousands of guns seemed to be firing, both big and little. I saw a grand sight! Looking over fairly level country every hedge was spitting flame, and about two miles away our shells were bursting in one of the two captured villages, sending up huge clouds of black and white smoke, and clouds of pink brick dust. It was a grand sight!

On the 4th I visited one or two cemeteries. Our guns were still going at top speed. In the afternoon a telegram came requesting me to take a photograph of an unknown wounded man at a clearing station near us. I was sent off straight away and took ten photos of him. He was quite unconscious and was not expected to come conscious again. Haddon tells me the photos have come out well, so I hope they will be of use.

The fifth was quite an exciting day. Just at breakfast time Fritz landed a bomb or two on a trainload of ammunition about half a mile away. It was a sight! I was looking out of our window. First some cordite flared up with a bright yellow flame, the fire caught some rifle ammunition which went off with a merry crack, then the heavier stuff caught! My! It went off truckload by truckload and took nearly all day to burn. Huge clouds of smoke went up thousands of feet in the air, and crash! the explosions fairly rocked the town about. Windows were falling all over the place. It sounded like a bull in a china shop. An impromptu military band was got together and marched up and down the street to calm the inhabitants.

Later in the morning I went out to various cemeteries and got a fine view of one of the biggest explosions. It looked like a huge black mushroom. Our bedroom was all covered by plaster and dust when we got back.

On the 6th I went to Boulogne to obtain some pegs, and had an hour or two with Athel. He is very different to when I saw him last – ever so much more cheerful and looks in better health altogether. We got caught in a big storm on the way over the hills and got very wet. In the evening it cleared up a bit. Our guns were going a bit but nothing out of the ordinary. Early in the morning I woke feeling something was wrong. The floor seemed to be moving under me as though I was on board ship. The whole house seemed to move. Curiously enough we felt rather than heard the mines go up. In a few seconds our guns began altogether with a crash, and then for an hour there was one steady roar like a big waterfall. We jumped up and all looked out of the window to see the hills lit up with the flash of our guns, and little scintillations all along where the shrapnel was bursting. Old Fritz had the wind up – as well he might, and was sending up repeated signals – two red lights, then some white ones, then a green one and a whole display of Very lights. Then all of a sudden the guns ceased, except for an occasional heavy, just to keep things going. First thing in the morning we heard the good news that everything was going ok and we had captured their third line. Then a stream of lorries, ambulances etc started down the street, carrying the wounded. Most of the wounds seemed pretty slight ones. There were not many stretcher cases. We saw one or two German wounded.

Later on in the day, to my surprise, a telegram came telling me to stand by ready to go back to Headquarters. In the afternoon I was taken back by car. I saw Haddon and heard that I had to come down here to clear up some of the back work. I specially asked that when I had done this I should be allowed to go back to section. I have had a good many months there with the Germans always getting in the way and interfering with my work, and I wanted to have the benefit of visiting some of the country which has been freed from their objectionable shells.

On the 10th I went round in the car to lots of little places within thirty miles of here, where one or two British soldiers have been buried. It was beautiful country and we had to find our way by map. One place we visited was very picturesque. It was the old fortress which withstood the British attack just before the battle of Crecy.

Yesterday was some big procession day for the French. All the houses here had white sheets hung outside them, and the road and paths were strewn with grass, leaves and flowers. All the little country places were the same. It was quite pretty.

> The children were dressed up – the girls in white kind of bridal costume, and the boys in black with a white rosette on their sleeves. There were impromptu shrines decked with flowers at various places in the villages, and at one place we passed the procession, which was a great show, but I didn't know what it was all about.
>
> Last night there was a very severe thunderstorm which woke us all up – like a bombardment. Today I have been engaged on clerical work – so here we are again up to date. I am hoping to get out of the railway part of the business and get everywhere by car. Please let Nurse read this letter as it is absolutely impossible for me to write another one like it. I am going to have a try at getting leave. Everybody seems to be going at Headquarters, and I have been fourteen months without one. I shall have to wait until I have finished this work though.

The Caterpillar Crater is one of two mines that were detonated by the Australian Tunnelling Company at Hill 60 and most resembles the crater in Ivan's photograph. It is hard to be sure, however, as the ground has changed significantly over the last century. The blast, from 70,000lb of ammonal, left 800 Germans dead.

A mine crater on Hill 60 on the south-east side of Ypres. It most resembles the Caterpillar Crater.

The Caterpillar Crater at Hill 60 in 2015. It was created by an explosive charge of 70,000lb of ammonal.

1918

The year 1918 saw the largest shifts in the front line since 1914. The Germans had maintained a largely defensive position since both sides entrenched in autumn 1914, leaving the allies to take the initiative in launching offensives. These offensives, such as the Somme and Passchendaele, made little gain relative to the huge number of casualties. By 1918 the Germans realized they had to launch an all-or-nothing offensive to win the war before the Americans showed up in force. Their forces had also increased by fifty divisions on the Western Front following the capitulation of Russia in 1917, affording them a temporary numerical advantage. The Germans began their big push forward – the *Kaiserschlacht* ('Kaiser's Battle') – on 21 March which initially made massive gains. The first operation was called MICHAEL, focused on the Somme; the second was called GEORGETTE which began on 9 April on the south side of the

Ypres Salient, attacking places such as Armentières, Bailleul and Kemmel. Allied gains made by the bloody sacrifice of 1917 were lost and more.

In January 1918 Ivan lived in a dugout in Dickebusch and then was based around Poperinghe and Ypres as the German offensive got under way and allied forces were forced to withdraw in many areas:

> In 1918, the last year of the war, this became very noisy as the Germans tried to advance in many places. Our leave was stopped. Our work was extra difficult and sometimes very dangerous. At Poperinghe I lived in a cellar for two days while it was being shelled. Then I moved up to Ypres Prison where the dressing station was being shelled by armour piercing shells. All too busy to be comfortable.

Here are some entries from his 1918 diary:

> **9.1.18** Very cold. Pack up kit. Cycle to Dickebusch. Take photos in Huts Cemetery. Heavy fall of snow in afternoon. Take up abode in dug-out. Receive postal order. Play whist.
>
> **10.1.18** All snow disappeared. Work in huts all the morning. (Plenty of shrapnel going off.) Work in Mty. Cemetery in afternoon. See Jack passing by and speak to him. 100 exp. Write letters etc. in evening.
>
> **22.1.18** Car to Shrapnel Corner. Walk to Railway Dugouts. Take 50. Rather lively with AA duds etc. Clerical work in afternoon. Evening as usual.
>
> **24.1.18** Car to Voormezeele, walk by Touseys track to Spoilbank. Then along trench railway to the Bluff, Hedge Row Cemetery and Woods Mty. Cemetery. Very lively. Have to come back quick. Work at Bedford House. Clerical work in afternoon.
>
> **25.1.18** Car to Bus House. Take photos and at Shelly Farm. Take a few at Voormezeele, Elzenwalle Château and Brewery. Very lively few minutes in afternoon. 5 shells very close to dugout. See balloon break adrift and parachutes used.
>
> **18.3.18** Fine day. Cycle to Lijssenthoek. Shells come fairly close on Abeele Road. Take 100 exp. Giles goes on leave. Clerical work in afternoon. Evening as usual.

19.3.18 Shells all night. Wet morning. Shells all morning. Offices, club, square etc. shelled in afternoon [in Poperinghe]. Work in cellar. Evening at billet.

20.3.18 Write Joan birthday. Billet shelled. Remove kit to cellar. Work at Lijssenthoek in afternoon. Sleep – or try to sleep in cellar.

21.3.18 Fine day, but shelly. Cycle to Godewaersveldt and spend afternoon on Mont des Cats. Shells from 7 pm to 8 am. No sleep.

22.3.18 Cycle to Reninghelst, Bailleul and Locre and spend afternoon on Mont des Cats. Very horrible night. No sleep.

23.3.18 Cycle to Ypres. Take photos at Prison cemetery. Take up abode in the Prison. Sleep from 8pm to 8am.

1.4.18 Prison shelled in the morning. Capt. Jewel visits in morning. Return to unit at Lijssenthoek in afternoon. Pub etc. in the evening.

Prison Cemetery (later Ypres Reservoir Cemetery), Ypres. Ivan has taken this picture from within the prison grounds with the cemetery visible through the rubble of the rear wall, looking northwards. The reservoir lies just beyond the cemetery.

At this point Ivan moved to the field hospital next to Lijssenthoek Military Cemetery. Here photography took a back seat while he acted as an orderly doing all sorts of odd jobs, including X-ray work, digging graves and making crosses. He makes several references to the No. 2 Canadian Casualty Clearing Station which was located at Remy Siding at Lijssenthoek. On 14 April No. 2 CCS and others had to withdraw due to the German advance. He recalls in his memoirs and diary:

> I moved to a hut in Lijssenthoek Cemetery, Poperinghe, and the Germans began to advance on the Ypres sector and captured Kemmel and Bailleul. In one day what had been a casualty clearing station with nurses and operating theatre, X Ray dept. etc. became an advanced dressing station with walking wounded pouring in. We could see the guns firing on the hills around Locre. I was commanded to dig a grave for 20 men. Then all personnel like us were withdrawn further away from the line and I then lived on the farm at Esquelbecq and moved to as many cemeteries as I could reach on the push bike. The advance was stopped and the Germans pushed right back on the Ypres front.
>
> **9.4.18** Early morning walk. Attack begins on Armentières. Do nothing all day. Concert at Y.M.C.A. evening.
>
> **10.4.18** Early morning walk. Hear of German advance at Armentières and Steenwerke. Walk to Boeschepe and have tea. Terrible lot of wounded come into LO.CCS. Major Faire calls in the evening.
>
> **11.4.18** Heavy misty day. Terrible lot of wounded arrive. See X-ray work in hospital. Dig a grave in the afternoon. Walk in the evening.
>
> **12.4.18** Walk in morning. Plenty of aerial activity. Dig a grave in the morning. X-ray work afternoon and evening. Interesting cases. Sgt. Callow and many others arrive from sections.
>
> **13.4.18** Lively night. Make crosses in morning. X-ray work in afternoon. Evening as usual. Hear of move to Dozinghem.
>
> **14.4.18** Dull, cold and windy. No.10 and No.2 Cdn. CCS move [No. 2 CCS moved to Esquelbecq]. We start moving but it is cancelled. Everything now disquietens. Service at Y.M.C.A. in evening.

15.4.18 Scrounge around all day. Dull weather. Hear of coming changes in G.R.U. Play chess in the evening.

16.4.18 Dull morning. Hawkes and Newell go to Abbeville. Goddard and Giles arrive back in afternoon. Troops everywhere. Guns firing everywhere. Have drink in the evening.

17.4.18 Dull day. Goddard and Giles leave Poperinghe for Abbeville under trying circumstances. Odd jobs all day. Sleep in dugout.

On 22 April 1918 he writes to Viola:

First I shall mention that I have moved, but not with No. 6 Unit as I expected. I have gone to No. 3 Unit which is now situated at a place not far away from the hospital where I was staying [this was at St Jan ter Biezen just west of Poperinghe]. The address is No. 3 M.G.R.Unit c.o. D.A.D.G.R.&E., 2nd Army. Please communicate this to all concerned. We have been having some extra special nights lately owing to the bright moon. The less said about them the better. [The 'bright moon' likely refers to the high amount of enemy action at the time. A bright moon would have increased night visibility thereby facilitating offensive activity such as air-raids and artillery fire.]

23/04/18 I hope very much that this year will see the last of this horrible war, but at present it is very awful. We have had two dull nights and last night it rained hard. Tonight it is fine again. I have got a good supply of films and have been out at work all day.

24/04/18 Not at all a bad night in spite of the moon. It is dull and misty this morning. I am staying with No. 3 section because it is nearer to my work than No. 6 now. No. 6 has gone miles away and, curiously enough are staying at the village where we were at Christmas 1915 [probably Arques]. I expect I shall go over there now and then to do some of the back, back work.

28.4.18 Clerical work all day. Walk in wood in evening. Heavy bombardment in evening.

8.5.18 Cycle early to Canada Farm via Rousbrugge and Crombeke. See German machine brought down in flames. Take 102 exp. at Canada Farm. Visit Ferme Olivier. Notes in afternoon. Visit village in evening.

30.5.18 Fine day. Spend day at Lijssenthoek (go by car). Take 120 exp. Plenty of shrapnel after balloons etc. Steenvoorde and Abeele look a bit smashed up. Afternoon and evening as usual.

On 30 May 1918 he wrote to Viola about Lijssenthoek Cemetery:

This morning I went by car to the big cemetery where the hospital used to be at which I lived for a time in April. Everything has changed and there is a war on there now. The cemetery is very much overgrown with weeds (it used to be one of our show places). I did a lot of work there and the weather was splendid. Coming back we watched some of our sausages being attacked. I have been quite busy for two days but have now run out of films again.

7.6.18 Cycle to Nine Elms. Take 20. Too lively to go to Poperinghe. Concert at No.2 C.C.S. in afternoon. Village in the evening.

Aside from discovering the odd shell hole in a cemetery, Ivan does not mention any more problems with shellfire beyond June 1918. By July the German offensive had run out of steam – having inflicted and suffered severe losses – the Americans had arrived in droves, the allies were finally breaking four years of deadlock and pushing forward to ultimate victory.

Ivan would make it through the war unscathed bar one incident flagged up in his medical record on 3 September 1916. It states that he was admitted to hospital having sustained a 'wound of face...of a trivial nature...at some cross roads on the main road to Boulogne about 12 km from the town of Hesdin whilst proceeding in a motor car to cemeteries at Étaples and Boulogne to photograph graves of soldiers buried.' This injury appears to have been an accident, most likely involving the car, rather than the result of enemy action.

Chapter Five

The Cemeteries: Then and Now

In Flanders fields the poppies blow
Between the crosses, row on row,
That mark our place; and in the sky
The larks, still bravely singing, fly
Scarce heard amid the guns below.
We are the Dead. Short days ago
We lived, felt dawn, saw sunset glow,
Loved and were loved, and now we lie,
In Flanders fields.
Take up our quarrel with the foe:
To you from failing hands we throw
The torch; be yours to hold it high.
If ye break faith with us who die
We shall not sleep, though poppies grow
In Flanders fields.

John McCrae

Anyone visiting the First World War battlefields in France and Belgium can still find mine craters, landscapes undulating where shells tore up the ground, concrete bunkers, and in some places trenches have been preserved. Tonnes of shell cases and other relics of war are still churned up each year. However, it is clear that one feature shows up more than anything else: the numerous Commonwealth cemeteries dotted around the countryside.

During the First World War 956,703 soldiers of the British Empire were killed in action, died of wounds, disease or injury, or were missing presumed dead. Of this number 564,715 died in France and Flanders. The Ypres Salient has 160 cemeteries and French Flanders has 331 cemeteries. Ivan's diaries and photos show that he visited a great many of these.

Signs of the Imperial War Graves Commission at the Lille Gate in Ypres.

Most cemeteries were in close proximity to the front-line battlefields and fairly makeshift in design, while others were attached to casualty clearing stations and field hospitals much further behind the lines and contained the graves of men who had succumbed to their wounds. Those closer to the battlefields were often very hard to locate as they, and any surrounding features including the roads, may have been severely damaged or even obliterated by shelling. For this reason it became more desirable, where possible, to transfer the remains of fallen soldiers to the larger cemeteries further behind the lines.

The state of the battlefields and cemeteries came as quite a shock to Sir Edwin Lutyens, one of the distinguished architects who designed many of the cemeteries after the war, when he visited the Western Front in 1917. He got to see the challenge that lay ahead with his own eyes and eloquently described the graves in a letter to his wife dated 12 July:

> The 'cemeteries' – the dotted graves – are pathetic, especially when one thinks how things are run and problems treated at home. What humanity can endure, suffer, is beyond belief. The battlefields – the obliteration of all human endeavour, achievement, and the human achievement of destruction, is bettered by poppies

> and wild flowers – that are as friendly to an unexploded shell as they are to the leg of a garden seat in Surrey.
>
> One is seeing very little of all there is to be seen – we are not allowed very near the front, but that little is ominous of what lies beyond. A battlefield with blurred trenches, the position of a machine gun marked by its litter of spent cartridges, the ruined tanks, the rough broken shell-hole pitted ground you assume was once a village, where a small bit of wall of what once was a church may stand but nothing else.
>
> The half ruined places are more impressive, for then you can picture what a place might have been. The grave-yards, haphazard from the needs of much to do and little time for thought – and then a ribbon of isolated graves like a milky way across miles of country, where men were tucked in where they fell – Ribbons of little crosses each touching each across a cemetery – set in a wilderness of annuals, – and where one sort of flower has grown the effect is charming, easy, and oh so pathetic, that one thinks no other monument is needed.
>
> For miles these graves occur, from single graves to close-packed areas of thousands, on every sort of site and in every sort of position – the bodies laid to face the enemy – in some places so close one wonders how to arrange their names in decent order. (*Life of Lutyens*, p.373.)

It was the responsibility of each regiment to bury its own dead, often very close to where they fell or not far behind the front line. Some units would endeavour to bury their dead as closely together as possible in the same cemetery; this is particularly apparent in Vlamertinghe Military Cemetery where, for example, the King's Liverpool Regiment has 118 burials. The chaplain or officer who had buried a fallen soldier was required to report the position of the grave to the DGR&E. Then GRU personnel could visit the grave to verify it, register all particulars and ensure that it was marked by a durable wooden cross. However, in the chaos of war it was commonplace for graves to become lost or isolated. When ground changed hands some allied graves would inevitably become situated behind enemy lines and might even mingle with graves of the enemy.

Ivan would often go out searching for, or would happen upon, isolated graves as he moved around the front-line areas of Flanders, taking the opportunity to register and photograph them. The only time Ivan recorded having to dig graves himself was during the German advance of 1918 when the military situation was at its most critical.

The following excerpts, taken from Ivan's 1917–19 diaries, are mostly from around the Ypres Salient:

1.3.17 Spring day. Go to Steenwerck Com, Trois Arbres, Nieppe, Romarin, Maple Leaf and isolated grave. In afternoon do clerical work.

14.3.17 Wet day. Go to Poperinghe and L'Ebbe Farm in morning. Search for odd grave. Clerical work for remainder of day. Evening as usual.

7.5.17 Cycle to Fleurbaix and then with Cpl. Cotman to Rue de Bois, Rue Petillon along Rue David to cemetery. 10 isolated graves and then Wye Farm and back to Fleurbaix and Estaires. Very warm riding. Clerical work in afternoon. Sit in garden in the evening.

28.7.17 Find that photo set has gone to Watou. In morning go to Steenwerck, Nieppe, Neuve Eglise, Wulverghem, Lindenhoek. See the battle field and crater and find stray graves. Cycle to Watou in afternoon. On return find Stapley waiting. Spend evening with him and see Jack at his camp. Sleep out.

3.8.17 Go to Voormezeele in car and walk to Moated Grange. Then along old front-line finding stray graves. Horribly wet and muddy. In afternoon do odd jobs. Sleep at billet.

8.8.17 Go out to Kemmel district and search for graves in morning. Take photos at Kleine Vierstraat. Spend afternoon at office. Hot bath, phonograph etc. in evening. Alleman over at 4 am [German air-raid]. Return to cellar. Camera stand and parcel from nurse arrive.

9.8.17 Go to R.E. Farm and Rest-and-be-thankful Farm. Find odd graves. Then to Kleine Vierstraat and Vierstraat and find more graves. Take photos in Bailleul in afternoon. More rain. Pub in evening. Sleep in barn at night.

The grave of Private W.D. Clark of the Canadian 29th Battalion, killed in action on 13 October 1915, at Wulverghem Lindenhoek Road Cemetery just to the west of Messines. This image was enlarged from a VPK negative.

12.8.17 Cycle out and find stray grave at Croix de Poperinghe. Write letters in field. Lounge about in afternoon. Go to service at Y.M.C.A. in evening. Sleep out at farm. Feel big concussion in morning.

5.9.17 Car to Salvation Corner. Then to Bard Cottage, Bridge 6A and Talana Farm. Walk over Yser to Glimpse Cottage, Lancs Farm and other places. Find many new graves. Visit Foch Farm. Return to Bard Cottage. Work in office and in Bailleul in afternoon. Sleep in cellar. Big bombardment in night and thunder storms.

8.9.17 Car to Ypres Prison. Car through Lille Gate and walk to China Wall Garden Farm and Half-way House. Return via Hellfire Corner. Record 85 graves. Work in office in afternoon. Sleep in cellar.

10.9.17 Car to Ypres then by Lille Gate to Shrapnel Corner. Walk to Dugouts and Zillebeke and return along north bank of lake. Find 167 graves. See red balloon floating. Sleep in cellar.

Isolated graves at Messines. The wooden cross in the centre marks the grave of Rifleman Arthur Egbert Gerrard, 'B' Company, 13th Battalion King's Royal Rifle Corps. Next to him is the grave of Lance Corporal H.J. Palmer of the same battalion. Both were killed in action on 1 July 1917. The graves were moved to Messines Ridge British Cemetery after the armistice.

23.10.17 Wet morning. Cycle out to Rhineboom and take isolated grave. Odd jobs for remainder of the day. Write to Phyllis and E.P.P.

19.1.18 Cycle to Brandhoek. Take 120. Hear big 15-inch gun fired. Dull day. Take one odd grave near the Huts. Clerical work late and letter writing.

23.1.18 Car to Shrapnel Corner. Walk to Railway Dug-outs. Take 50. Take some odd graves near Swan Château. In afternoon cycle to Hengebaert Farm, the Huts, Dickebusch Mty. Clerical work late.

28.3.18 Car to Cheddar Villa, St Julian. Work at Oxford Road, odd graves Wieltje, Wieltje Farm, and White House, St Jean. Walk back to Prison. Clerical work in afternoon.

27.9.18 Fine and windy. Cycle to Abeele Aerodrome, then to No.4 Section and Godewaersveldt. Then find two odd graves towards Mont des Cats. Clerical work etc. Medcalf goes to Wormhoudt.

20.11.18 Damp and foggy all day. Cycle to Morbecque Mty., Le Grand Hazard, isolated grave, Cinq-Rues and Le Peuplier. Cycle along railway. Clerical work until 8.30.

18.3.19 MC to Ypres, then via Gheluvelt to Zandvoorde. Bad roads. Search for graves and return via Hill 60. Work late.

Then and Now

The following set of photographs is of various cemeteries that Ivan visited, mostly around the Ypres Salient, showing how they looked then compared with now. Some were front-line cemeteries, some 'Base and Lines' cemeteries, and others concentration cemeteries that were created or vastly increased after the armistice.

Vlamertinghe Military Cemetery

Vlamertinghe is located about 2 miles west of Ypres. The cemetery was originally started by French troops in 1914 and then by Commonwealth troops from April 1915. Fighting units and field ambulances used it until June 1917 when the construction of a military railway alongside the cemetery precluded further extension. After the armistice the French graves were removed and the cemetery now contains 1,175 burials from the First World War.

Ivan's photograph blended with mine. The shell-damaged building is the Holy Family Chapel which was used as a dressing station during the war and soldiers who died of wounds were buried next to it. The building was rebuilt and is now used by the 'Chiro' (Flemish youth movement).

Two photos creating a not-quite-seamless panorama of the cemetery with the Holy Family Chapel on the left side and the ruined church on the right.

Poperinghe New Military Cemetery

The town of Poperinghe has two military cemeteries: the New and the Old. These photographs show the New Cemetery which was started in June 1915 around the time Ivan arrived in France. There are 677 Commonwealth soldiers and 271 French soldiers buried here.

Looking from the cemetery towards the main square. The church of St Bertin can be seen to the left and the town hall a little to its right.

A similar angle today.

Ramparts Cemetery

One of only two Commonwealth military cemeteries within the city limits of Ypres, Ramparts Cemetery can be found next to the Lille Gate on the south side. The other is Ypres Reservoir Cemetery. The Lille Gate is clearly visible to the right in Ivan's photograph and obscured by lush greenery today. It was begun by the French in November 1914 and was then used by Commonwealth troops on and off from February 1915 to April 1918. There are 198 Commonwealth soldiers buried here.

Ypres Reservoir Cemetery

This cemetery was originally called Cemetery North of the Prison due to its proximity to the prison, and then Ypres Reservoir North Cemetery. Ypres Reservoir Middle and South Cemeteries were then moved to the North Cemetery and the name changed to Ypres Reservoir Cemetery. The name change apparently was to avoid any unfortunate misunderstandings as to why soldiers were buried so close to the prison.

The cemetery was started in October 1915 and used throughout the war. Graves from a small cemetery at the Infantry Barracks were also moved here after the armistice, along with a number of graves brought in from nearby battlefields. There are 2,613 Commonwealth soldiers buried or commemorated here, of which 1,034 are unidentified.

Looking towards the Cross of Sacrifice and Stone of Remembrance.

The cemetery c.1919 with the ruins of the Cathedral and Cloth Hall in the distance. The back wall of the prison, damaged by shellfire, is visible on the right-hand side. New dwellings can be seen on the Plaine d'Amour.

The cemetery in August 2015, facing away from the prison.

The Ypres Reservoir full. The ruins of the prison can be seen to the right and a ribbon of grave markers can be made out across the centre of the image.

Essex Farm Cemetery

Blend of Ivan's photograph with mine showing the canal bank running behind the cemetery.

Essex Farm Cemetery is located in Boesinghe on the north side of Ypres, and was started from a dressing station in April 1915. It sits in front of the Yser Canal bank which was just behind the front line in 1915. Consequently, it was frequently under fire and one of the more dangerous cemeteries visited by Ivan. Lieutenant Colonel John McCrae of the Canadian Army Medical Corps was stationed here when he famously penned the poem *In Flanders Fields* in May 1915.

These concrete bunkers are next to the cemetery and were used to shelter from artillery fire. They evolved from dugouts cut into the spoil bank from the Yser Canal that were used as a medical post and advanced dressing station.

There are 1,200 Commonwealth soldiers buried or commemorated here, of which 103 are unidentified.

The headstone of the youngest casualty I have come across while photographing war graves: Rifleman Valentine Joe Strudwick who was killed by a shell on 16 January 1916, aged just 15. It is estimated that about 250,000 'boy soldiers' under the age of 18 fought for Britain during the First World War.

Railway Dugouts Burial Ground (Transport Farm)

Railway Dugouts Burial Ground lies to the south of Ypres. It is easily accessed by passing through the Lille Gate and then heading east at a turning named Shrapnel Corner, towards Zillebeke Lake.

Many of the burials are from 1916 and 1917 when advanced dressing stations were operating out of the dugouts and the farm. The cemetery was frequently shelled. There are 2,459 Commonwealth soldiers buried or commemorated here, of which 430 are unidentified.

The grave of Lieutenant George Walter Nation, of the 7th Battalion Canadian Infantry, at Railway Dugouts. He was killed in action on 25 July 1916 when the Germans detonated a mine at the Bluff, near Hill 60 in the Ypres Salient. He was aged 21. The cemetery appears to be in disarray with crosses leaning at different angles and resembles a swamp with all the mud and water.

Railway Dugouts in 2015.

Bedford House Cemetery

Bedford House is the name given by the army to Rosendal Château, the remains of which can be seen within the cemetery. The cemetery was frequently subjected to shellfire, as is clearly depicted in Ivan's photograph (see p. 62), resulting in the gradual and total destruction of the château. It lies on the south side of Ypres, near Zillebeke, and is one of the most beautiful Commonwealth cemeteries that I have visited. It is like a large English garden with its great variety of attractive plants and shrubs.

The cemetery consists of four enclosures that now contain 5,139 burials of which 3,011 are unidentified. A large number of the graves were brought in from around the Ypres Salient after the armistice. One enclosure was formed as remains were still being found in the 1930s and then sixty-nine soldiers of the Second World War were also buried here.

The Cloth Hall and Cathedral in Ypres can be made out in the distance.

Kemmel Château Military Cemetery

The cemetery was started in 1914 in the grounds of Kemmel Château, north-east of Kemmel village. The village and the cemetery were taken by the Germans during their advance in April 1918 and were subsequently shelled, severely damaging the cemetery and totally destroying the château. Ivan visited this cemetery on numerous occasions. The cemetery contains 1,131 Commonwealth burials from the First World War.

The cemetery with grave markers for Canadians Private D.Walsh, Private O. Frijs and Private F.C. Whitcutt. All were killed in action in November 1915. Private Frijs, who was a count of Danish origin, was killed by a sniper while repairing a parapet.

The same graves in 2015.

Then and now: the grave of Irishman Lance Corporal P.J. Barden, 6th Connaught Rangers, killed in action on 19 February 1917.

Maple Copse Cemetery

The small cemetery of Maple Copse lies close to Sanctuary Wood in the commune of Zillebeke in the Ypres Salient. There was an advanced dressing station here with burials dating from 1915 to 1917. Most of the graves are from 1916 which in this sector saw the Battle of Mount Sorrel in June. Due to its proximity to fierce front-line fighting, the cemetery was repeatedly shelled and many of the graves were obliterated. This is evident in Ivan's photograph and highlights how important it was to record as much information as possible about the particulars of graves.

Shell holes and splintered trees were principal features of Maple Copse Cemetery.

Maple Copse in 2015. These headstones are for Canadian men killed in 1916.

After the war the cemetery was transformed into a secluded oasis of tranquillity and beauty; a striking contrast to the desolation shown in Ivan's photographs. Many of the headstones, such as the Canadian graves shown in my picture, had to be marked 'Known to be buried in this cemetery' as the original grave markers had been destroyed. This inscription can be found at a number of other front-line cemeteries such as Railway Dugouts Burial Ground (Transport Farm) in the Ypres Salient. There are 308 Commonwealth soldiers buried or commemorated in this cemetery, of which only 78 could be located. Of these 78, only 26 were identified.

Hooge Crater Cemetery

The area around Hooge was blasted into a featureless wasteland. Since the war it has returned to its natural state of woods and farmland. The cemetery takes its name from the huge mine crater that was detonated by British Royal Engineers on 19 July 1915.

The cemetery was started in October 1917 and originally contained seventy-six burials. After the armistice it was massively enlarged when numerous graves were transferred here from smaller cemeteries around the Zillebeke, Zantvoorde and Gheluvelt battlefields. The number of soldiers buried or commemorated in this cemetery now totals 5,916 with as many as 3,570 unidentified.

The stone of remembrance is located in a sunken circle of lawn that represents the 1915 crater. The original crater was filled in.

A view of the cemetery looking north towards the Menin Road and a similar view in 2015. Just across the Menin Road are the Hooge Craters and the German lines where trenches, pill-boxes and bunkers can still be seen today (see Chapter 9 for more photographs of Hooge).

Tyne Cot Cemetery

Tyne Cot Concentration Cemetery, Passchendaele, was to become the largest British and Commonwealth military cemetery in the world, containing the burials or commemoration of 11,962 Commonwealth soldiers, of which 8,374 are unidentified. The cemetery was started in October 1917 following the capture of a large pill-box, visible in the background of Ivan's photograph, which was then used as an advanced dressing station. The name of the cemetery comes from a nearby barn that was dubbed 'Tyne Cottage' by the Northumberland Fusiliers. After the armistice the cemetery was vastly increased as remains were brought in from various small burial grounds and exhumations from the surrounding battlefields of Passchendaele and Langemark (also known as 'Langemarck'). Panels on the north-eastern boundary of the cemetery display the names of nearly 35,000 servicemen who have no known grave. This memorial to the missing was added when it became clear that the Menin Gate Memorial in Ypres would not have sufficient space for all the names.

The large pill-box was later covered over by the Cross of Sacrifice at the suggestion of King George V while touring the war cemeteries of the Western Front in May 1922. At the end of his tour the king famously remarked:

> We can truly say that the whole circuit of the Earth is girdled with the graves of our dead. In the course of my pilgrimage, I have many times asked myself whether there can be more potent advocates of peace upon Earth through the years to come, than this massed multitude of silent witnesses to the desolation of war.

A similar view in 2013 showing the Cross of Sacrifice covering the bunker. The panels displaying the names of the missing can be seen beyond.

Buttes New British Cemetery, Polygon Wood

Polygon Wood lies to the south of Zonnebeke in the Ypres Salient and was totally destroyed during the war. This burial ground was made following the armistice as numerous graves from the Zonnebeke battlefields were transferred here. There are 2,108 soldiers buried or commemorated here, of which 1,677 are unidentified.

Above is a photographic blend showing the Australian memorial on the Butte. Ivan's picture shows devastation that has now been replaced by woods and a walled walkway to the cemetery which lies to the right of the Butte. The memorial is dedicated 'To the Officers and Non-Commissioned Officers and men of the fifth Australian Division who fought in France and Belgium, 1916, 1917, 1918.' The Butte was originally used as a firing range by the Belgian army.

The Australian memorial on the Butte and the cemetery.

Lijssenthoek Military Cemetery

Lijssenthoek is a hamlet very near to Poperinghe to the west of Ypres. It became a prime location for receiving the wounded of the Ypres Salient with its proximity to the front and to the Poperinghe-Hazebrouck railway, yet beyond the range of most German field artillery. At first there was a large French evacuation hospital called Remy Siding which from June 1915 was taken over by several Commonwealth casualty clearing stations. By 1917 the site comprised four CCS with 4,000 hospital beds and was the largest evacuation hospital in the Ypres Salient. Those that succumbed to their wounds were buried in the cemetery which grew to be the second-largest Commonwealth cemetery in Belgium with 10,784 burials. This number includes 883 graves of other nationalities, mostly French and German.

Due to its size and location in a back area it is not surprising that this was the cemetery most visited and photographed by Ivan, and at one point he was even living in a hut here. He helped out doing X-ray work here in April 1918 when the Germans pushed forward, until all CCS personnel consequently had to withdraw and were replaced by field ambulances.

Gardeners at work in Lijssenthoek Cemetery.

GRU personnel Sheppard and Newell at the doorway of a Nissen hut in Lijssenthoek.

This cemetery is very densely populated.

A headstone marking the graves of two German soldiers, one *unbekannter* (unknown).

Wimereux Communal Cemetery

Ivan's photograph blended with mine. Due to the sandy nature of the soil, the headstones had to be laid flat.

Wimereux is about 3 miles north of Boulogne where several military hospitals were based during the war. The cemetery was used by various medical units for burials from October 1914 to June 1918. It contains 2,847 Commonwealth burials from the First World War, including Lieutenant Colonel John McCrae who died of pneumonia on 28 January 1918. There is also a plot of 170 German war graves.

The grave of John McCrae.

German Cemeteries

While in search of British and Commonwealth graves Ivan would inevitably happen upon German burial grounds too. It was not unusual for these to contain graves of British soldiers. In a letter to his mother dated October 1918 he writes about a trip into the Ypres Salient, heading down the Menin Road and beyond Gheluvelt:

> We searched a bit and discovered a large German cemetery. This had been kept beautifully with paths and flowers of all descriptions. We found several British graves. *These were treated in every way the same as their own men. Good wooden crosses with inscriptions properly painted and just the same arrangement of flowers. You see the Hun is not a Hun in every respect* [these words were italicized and underlined by Ivan.] It was a very interesting trip.

The only existing photograph of a German cemetery taken by Ivan was at Bazentin on the Somme. I cannot find any information about this cemetery and so it is most likely that the graves were transferred to the much larger German cemetery at Fricourt, 3 miles away.

German Cemetery at Bazentin, between Pozières and Longueval.

The entrance to Langemark Military Cemetery.

Stone tablets each mark the graves of several soldiers, some unknown.

The *Kameraden Grab* (the 'Comrades Grave'). Thousands of unidentified dead brought in from post-war battlefield exhumations are interred here, totalling 24,917. These bronze panels display the names of 17,342 soldiers whose remains have never been identified and it is believed, based on archive research, that those listed were buried in this mass grave.

A bronze sculpture of four soldiers mourning a fallen comrade.

There is a huge disparity in the numbers of Commonwealth and German cemeteries. In the Somme, for example, there are 410 Commonwealth cemeteries compared to only 14 German cemeteries. The reason for this huge contrast, given that both sides suffered similarly large losses, is that the Imperial War Graves Commission chose to maintain a great many of the small cemeteries and sought to provide an individual grave for every fallen soldier recovered. Only cemeteries with fewer than forty burials were absorbed into concentration cemeteries. The Germans, like the French, opted for mass burials and so all of the smaller cemeteries were absorbed into much larger ones.

When the armistice was signed the German equivalent of the GRUs was disbanded and care of German graves in France and Belgium was left to the respective authorities. In November 1919 the *Volksbund Deutsche Kriegsgräberfürsorge* (VDK) – the People's Association for the Care of German War Graves – came into being. Its work outside Germany was initially very restricted, having to comply with the victors' stipulations.

When I visited the German military cemetery at Langemark in the Ypres Salient I was struck by the stark contrast with Commonwealth cemeteries. The latter tend to be bright, open spaces of tranquillity with plenty of colour provided by a rich variety of flora. Langemark felt crepuscular and monotone, surrounded by many trees, with little in the way of flowers or shrubs. The crosses and stone tablets are all fashioned from a dark-toned basalt and tend to have several names on each.

The cemetery was begun in 1915 and contains the remains of more than 44,000 German soldiers. Ivan passed through Langemark several times in 1919, accessing the nearby Cement House Cemetery and Poelcapelle British Cemetery, and more than likely visited the German cemetery. Two British servicemen killed in 1918 are commemorated here.

Chapter Six

The Grief of a Nation

A rose among the headstones in Maple Copse Cemetery.

The manhood of Britain went off to war in 1914. Never before had so many men been enveloped in such a huge national effort, and never before had so many men been sacrificed for king and country. Mothers, wives and others up and down the country were handed the bombshell of a letter or telegram informing them of the death of a loved one at the front. Hardly a street would have been untouched by grief, such was the scale of loss. The war ultimately left more than 192,000 women as widows, nearly 360,000 children without fathers, and about half a million children lost siblings.

Many people were fortunate, relatively speaking, to receive letters from the front expressing deep sympathy and detailing what had happened to their loved ones, while others had very scant information.

Those who had received full details about the resting place of a loved one were often anxious about how the graves were being cared for and in many cases were clamouring for the repatriation of remains. The War Office had issued an official ban on repatriation in 1915. However, vast numbers of soldiers were classed as 'missing', leaving an unbearable ache of uncertainty. Naturally, many relatives were desperate for any information they could acquire. In late 1916 the Directorate of Graves Registration and Enquiries published a pamphlet entitled 'The Care of the Dead' designed to reassure the public of what was being done in respect of soldiers' graves. The final paragraph reads:

> In all wars it has been one of the fears haunting a soldier's friends that his body may be utterly lost. Even in this war there have been such irretrievable losses. But in no great war has so much been done as in this, to prevent the addition of that special torment to the pains of anxiety and of bereavement.

Being able to visit the grave of the deceased is a normal part of the process of mourning the loss of a loved one. It provides an opportunity to say goodbye and helps meet a natural need for closure. In 1978 my uncle Ian Gordon-Smith and his wife and two children were all killed in a tragic road accident while serving as missionaries in Thailand. Later that year my parents travelled to Thailand to visit the place where the accident happened and the cemetery where they were buried. My father in particular needed to better grasp what had happened in order to grieve for his brother who had been 'wrenched from him'. During the Great War this type of trip largely wasn't possible for relatives back home as the dead were mostly buried too close to the front line and no one could predict when the slaughter would finally end. Some cemeteries under British control found themselves under German control as the front line shifted. Graves were recorded as carefully as possible by men such as Ivan, but continued fighting and shelling often destroyed the grave markers and once things had quietened there might be nothing left in a newly-churned-up landscape.

Ivan's job facilitated a way for families to mourn their loved ones who had lost their lives in the line of duty. His work provided relatives with something tangible of what remained of their loved one; a window they could not otherwise have had, at least not until well after the termination of hostilities.

Ivan himself would lose friends, relatives and acquaintances in the war. He inevitably would find himself photographing the grave of someone he knew. This happened at least three times.

The first was Sapper Frederick Grayling who worked for Kodak as a photographic checking clerk. He lived in Stoke Newington in north London with his wife Minnie and two daughters, and enlisted into the 1st London Company of the Royal Engineers (Territorial Force).

His unit joined the 6th Division in France on 23 December 1914, stationed at Bois Grenier and Erquinghem near Armentières. No major action took place in this sector during the period that Frederick was based here and casualties were relatively low, but the trenches were under the constant threat of shellfire and sniping. On 26 March

Sapper Grayling's grave (left side) in Cité Bon Jean Military Cemetery, Armentières.

1915 the company war diary notes: 'Works as usual. Spr Grayling No. 625 wounded.' The following day he 'died in hospital from septic wound' aged 25. He was buried in Cité Bon Jean Cemetery and his wife had the epitaph 'Sleep on beloved and take thy rest' inscribed on his headstone after the war. Ivan visited this cemetery numerous times throughout the war and recorded that he found Sapper Grayling's grave on 21 July 1915.

The second was Sergeant Harry Richard Daniels of the 130th Field Company, Royal Engineers, who was part of the Sutton Congregational Boys' Life Brigade in which Ivan was also heavily involved. He grew up in Carshalton, Surrey and worked as an electrician and wireman prior to enlisting.

Harry's company entrained at Aldershot on 27 September 1915 to commence their journey over to France. Initially they were stationed around Nieppe and Armentières, and then around Ploegsteert. The company war diary shows that they were mainly involved in 'working parties' carrying out a range of tasks in the trenches such as revetting, salvage, work on dugouts, fire steps, breastworks, gas and machine-gun emplacements, and dismantling an old dressing station. They would work by day but often needed the cover of night if it was necessary to carry out work in more precarious conditions. The war diary shows that this sector was relatively quiet with little enemy attention and few casualties. However, on Friday, 14 January 1916 it reported: 'Between 40 & 50 whizzbangs were fired at St Yves in morning and 60 six inch shells in afternoon. Fortunately we had arranged night working. The trench was badly damaged east of Post Office.' In spite of this heavy barrage there were no casualties noted. The following day the diary reported: 'Working parties of 230 supplied. Work much the same as yesterday. Machine gun opened on 2nd relief in St Yves about 11pm and Sergt. H.R. Daniels was killed. One of the working party was killed and 2 wounded (Worcesters).' On 16 January the

The grave marker at the London Rifle Brigade Cemetery on the Rue d'Armentières. It states that Harry was killed in action on 15 January 1916 at St Yves Avenue, near Ploegsteert, aged 27.

diary noted: 'Sergt. H.R. Daniels was buried at 3pm in grave No. A.31 Rifle Bde. Cemetery, south end of Ploegsteert village by the Rev. D. Tail Patterson, Bde. Congregationalist Minister.'

The following newspaper cutting accompanies the photograph of his grave:

> A brief announcement was made last week of the death of Sergeant H.R. Daniels, of 4 Clifton Avenue, Belmont. Further particulars of his death have been received by his widow from the officers of his battalion, who speak of the great loss his death will cause and of the high regard and affection in which he was held by the men of his section. Mrs H.R. Daniels desires to thank the many friends who have written kind messages of sympathy with her in her great sorrow. Sergeant Daniels was a lieutenant in the Sutton Congregational Boys' Life Brigade, and will be much missed from among them. A memorial service will be held in the Congregational Church next Sunday after the morning service, at 12.15.

The headstone marking Harry's grave today. (*Courtesy of Alastair Baird*)

According to CWGC records, Harry was only the second man in his company to be killed, making his death seem all the more unfortunate. However, they would suffer many more casualties later in 1916 on the Somme.

Edgar Leonard Bawtree

Ivan's parents were from very large families, ensuring that he had numerous cousins. His much older cousin Julius Bawtree and wife Jane had a son called Edgar, who was born in London the same year as Ivan. The family lived in Purley, Surrey for many years and Edgar went to Christ's Hospital School in Horsham from 1905–10. They briefly lived at Clapham Lodge just before emigrating to Canada in September 1910.

They settled in Enderby, British Colombia, where Jane's family was living. Edgar enlisted here in 1916 and was shipped over to France later that year with the 46th Battalion of the Canadian Expeditionary Force. The battalion was engaged in action

Edgar in a school photo from summer 1910. He is in the middle row, second from left. (*Courtesy of Christ's Hospital School*)

around the northern end of the Arras sector, close to Vimy Ridge, in April and May 1917 and sustained heavy casualties (the 46th Battalion came to be known as the 'Suicide Battalion' as it suffered more than 90 per cent casualties). During the Battle of Vimy Ridge of 9–12 April the battalion was in action at Zouave Valley, between Souchez and Vimy Ridge. On 12 April they were part of a successful operation to take the northernmost part of the ridge, known as 'The Pimple'.

Edgar himself was wounded on 7 May at the Souchez River which runs between Lens and Vimy Ridge. The medical reports mostly say it was a gunshot wound which fractured his right thigh, although one mentions high explosive. He was operated on at a casualty clearing station which resulted in the removal of his right testicle. He was then moved to the No. 13 General Hospital in Boulogne and on 23 May he was shipped back to England and placed in the Metropolitan Hospital on the Kingsland Road in London.

Ivan does not mention Edgar in his surviving diaries and letters, which is curious since their families had had regular interaction and even lived together briefly. However, he does figure in a letter written by Athel to Viola on 23 May 1917. After two years in France Athel was clearly war-weary:

> We had a little rain again today and the sun at the same time – result – a rainbow. Now I get a little sentimental over that, and think of such lines as:-
>
> 'Appear, desire of Nations, Thine exiles long for home
> Show in the Heavens thy promised sign; Thou Prince and Saviour – Come.'
>
> [These lines are taken from the final verse of a hymn called *Ten Thousand Times Ten Thousand* by Henry Alford, 1867.]
>
> I am one of the exiles, and hope the rainbow indicates that the floods of War will surely abate before the whole world is engulfed.
>
> Oh I have just been told Edgar is gone to England this morning. I have not been able to see him since Sunday owing to duty – I feel rather sorry at that. His case would probably turn up at Brighton. If so, it might be a mutual good move for Aunt Polly to visit him there. Tell the rest this.

A preserved Canadian trench at Vimy Ridge, surrounded by shell holes. The 46th Battalion was posted to this sector at different points in April and May 1917.

Athel was stationed in Boulogne at the time and so was well-placed to visit Edgar. Sadly, it would be the last visit he would make as Edgar's condition deteriorated as the nasty wound to his groin became infected. He also had bed sores, abscesses and ran a temperature that remained between 100 and 106F. At times he was somewhat delirious and by late June he was 'dangerously ill'. The medical records that survive with his attestation papers are remarkably detailed. On 3 July 1917 he died from pyaemia (blood poisoning) and heart failure. We don't know which relatives were able to visit him in England and sadly it's unlikely that his parents would have been able to make it over from Canada in time.

As he died of wounds in London he was buried in Brookwood Military Cemetery in Surrey which has a large plot of Canadian graves. We do not know whether Ivan ever photographed the grave. If it was any consolation, at least he was buried with other Canadian soldiers close to where he grew up.

The grave of Edgar Bawtree at Brookwood Military Cemetery. The epitaph inscribed on the headstone is the words of Christ: 'I will come again, and receive you unto myself' (John 14:3).

Cousin Jack

Then in 1918 Ivan had to photograph the grave of one of his closer family members. His cousin Edmund Arthur Howe Lilley, known as Jack, was killed by shrapnel on the front between Arras and the Somme. Jack gets occasional mention in the diaries and he is the closest relative known to have been killed in action.

Ivan mentions spending time with Jack on three occasions in late July and early August 1917 in his diary. He had just moved to Bailleul and Jack's battalion was also camped nearby. In his memoirs he wrote:

> While at Bailleul (cousin) Jack came to see me and we spent an hour or two together. He spoke of the hectic life in the trenches and said it couldn't last long. A few months later he was killed by shell fire on the Somme and buried at St Amand Cemetery.

Jack was born on 21 November 1882 and was educated at Dulwich College from 1893–97. He then worked at the Harbour Works in Gibraltar for nine years. After this he settled down and worked in poultry and fruit-farming in Sussex. He married Annie Amelia Crockford in September 1907, a widow fourteen years his senior. He began his military training in May 1915 when he enlisted into the Territorial Force, joining the Inns of Court Officer Training Corps in Berkhamsted. He made an application for a temporary commission in the regular army for the duration of the war dated 23 August 1915, and the following month he was gazetted temporary second lieutenant in the 9th Battalion of the Bedfordshire Regiment which was based in Colchester. It remained in England as a reserve battalion from which men could be drafted into front-line units.

By this point we know from Viola's diary that Jack had separated from Annie and that she was nursing wounded soldiers. She states that in October 1915 Jack was ready to be sent to France any day, although his medal index card states it was not until May 1916.

Photo of Jack (date unknown) from the Dulwich College War Record 1914–19.

He was drafted into the 6th Battalion, part of the 112th Infantry Brigade attached to the 37th Division, which operated in various sectors of the Western Front during the war. However, on 29 June 1916 he was admitted to the No. 1 General Hospital at Le Havre having fallen ill with appendicitis. His battalion was based around Gommecourt at the time which was in the northernmost area of the Somme sector (about halfway between Arras and Albert). There is a telegram from the war office sent to his solicitors in Hastings requesting details of his next of kin and informing them of his illness dated 1 July, coinciding with the first day of the Somme offensive. It is probably just as well that the telegram went to his solicitors since telegrams during the war tended to inflict terror on the recipient as they were akin to the grim reaper knocking at one's door.

Once Jack had recovered he returned to France, presumably while the Battle of the Somme was still raging. While his battalion did not go over the top during the initial phase of the offensive it was engaged in later actions, including the Battle of Pozières in August and the Battle of the Ancre in November.

In 1917 Jack's battalion was engaged in the Arras offensive of April, and then moved north in preparation for the Third Battle of Ypres. On 1 July 1917 he was promoted to lieutenant. They were then engaged in fighting in particular around the Menin Road,

Polygon Wood, Broodseinde and Poelcapelle and remained in the Ypres Salient until the spring of 1918.

In February 1918 they were in front-line positions in the Menin Road sector until late March when the battalion entrained for the south and returned to the Gommecourt sector as the German Spring Offensive had got under way. This was a critical time for the British army, highlighted by Viola in her diary on 3 April: 'Letter from Jack to mater saying he's going to be in the thick of it, and can't write for a time.'

In May 1918 the men of the 6th Bedfordshire Battalion were transferred to the 1st/1st Hertfordshire Battalion (known as the 'Herts Guards'). We know that at some point after this, not long before his death, Jack was serving as acting captain in the Trench Mortar Battery (TMB).

In the early hours of the morning of 31 July Jack led the TMB on a mission to strafe the enemy trenches around Bucquoy in support of a raid. On that day the 112th Brigade War Diary reported:

> 1.15[am] We carried out a raid on the enemy trenches, N of Light Railway at F.28.6.8.0 & F.29.C.05.70. with artillery, M.G. & T.M. [Machine Gun & Trench Mortar] co-operation. The first objective (the enemy front line) was reached and found unoccupied.
>
> The raiding party was unable to proceed further owing to the enemy putting down a barrage between the first and second objectives.
>
> The 1st Battalion Essex Regiment carried out the raid. Their casualties were 1 officer (wounded), 3 ORs killed, 18 ORs wounded and 2 ORs missing (1 from previous patrol).

Strangely the diary fails to mention the one officer of the TMB killed during the raid, but Ivan received a letter from his friend Oswald Stapley, who was also in the Bedfordshire Regiment, which gives clear details of what happened to Jack that night:

> I was surprised and distressed by your note of 8th [August 1918] which I received yesterday afternoon, as soon as I came down from the line. As I wrote and told you, I spoke to Mr Lilley at Battalion HQ in the line on 29th and your note was the next news I had of him. I immediately went round to the TM HQ and there saw some of the fellows, one of whom was with your cousin when he was killed. It seems that on the night of the 31st our TMs were doing some strafing and for that purpose were moved up and came into action on an open road where there was no cover. About 1.30am Mr Lilley was standing by one of his guns and two fellows

were standing just in front of him, when a Fritz shell dropped about 20 yds from them. The other two noticed Mr Lilley fall, and bent down to see that a small piece of shrapnel had entered the left side of his head and passed through out of his helmet on the other side. He was killed instantly. A corporal of the TMB said, 'Capt. Lilley was one of the bravest men and best officers in the army', and the other chaps agreed. And I believe this was not just 'de mortem nil nisi bonum' for I've heard them express the same thoughts before. I found out where he was buried and went there last evening. It is a new little cemetery at a little village called – [St Amand]. There is no need to try to describe the cemetery to you – I'm afraid you know them only too well. It is a quiet spot between an orchard and the French cemetery.

Further information about Jack's death can be found in a letter from Second Lieutenant A.E. Hardy to his mother, Milena Lilley (Aunt Millie to Ivan):

St Amand British Cemetery. Jack's grave is in the front row, third from the left. The grave to the left of Jack's belongs to a soldier of the 1st Battalion of the Essex Regiment that carried out the trench raid in conjunction with Jack's trench mortar battery.

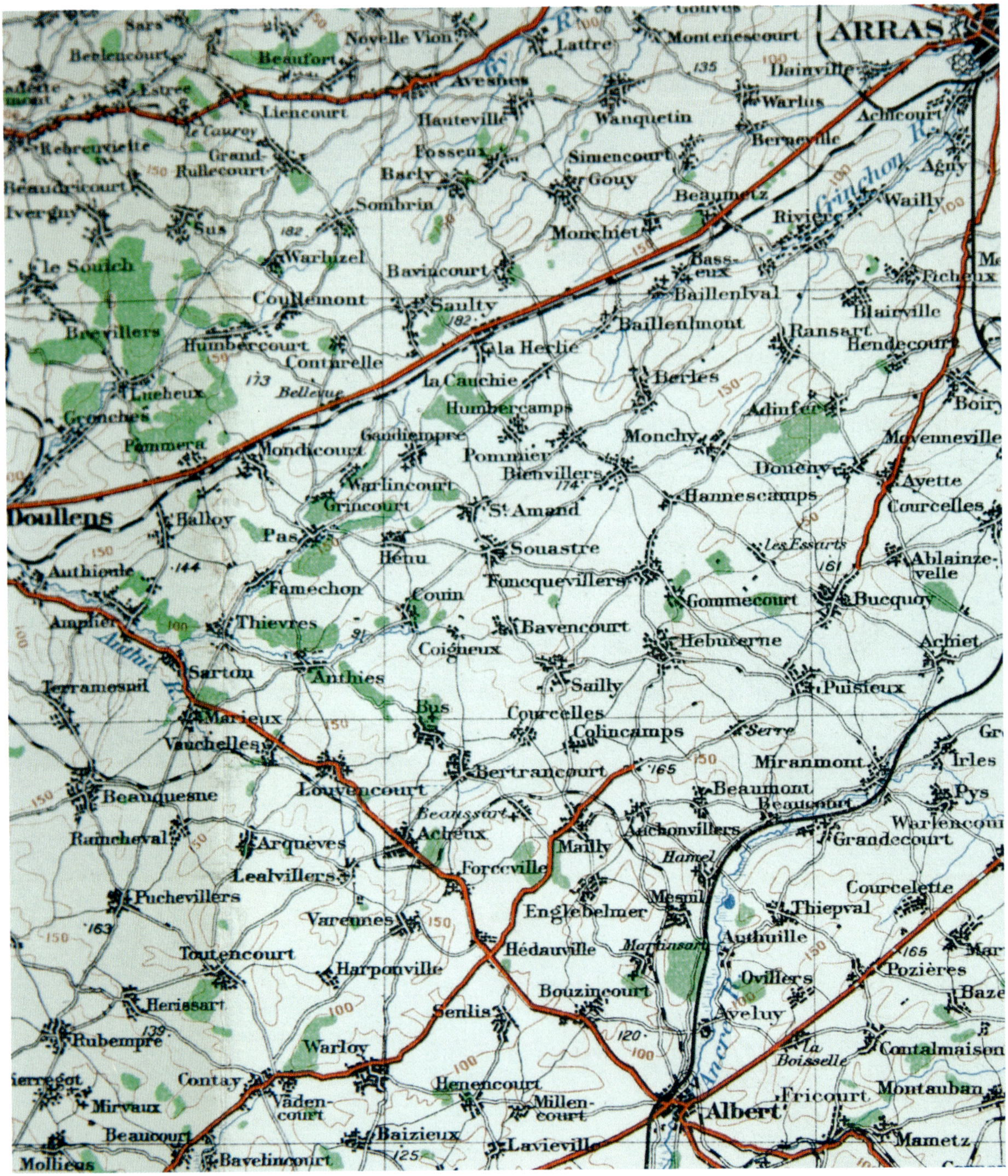

A section of a War Office map produced in February 1915 that belonged to Ivan showing the sector between Arras and Albert. St Amand is in the centre. Jack was killed at Bucquoy, near Gommecourt, on the centre-east side of the map.

The battery was engaged on special work, and rather than delegate the duty to a junior officer or an NCO he personally supervised the firing of the guns in order that he might encourage his men in a difficult situation.

He went to his duty cheerfully knowing that he had a difficult task. His men were encouraged by his presence; and were heartbroken by his death. He suffered no pain as his death was absolutely instantaneous. His death is regretted by both officers and men of the Battery who realise that they have not only lost a good commanding officer but also a true and loyal friend.

I am having all his kit and personal belongings collected and they will be forwarded to England through his Bankers Messrs Holt & Co.

Will you please accept my heartfelt sympathy for the loss of my dear friend your son.

These letters were fairly standard in format, emphasizing bravery, devotion to duty, popularity and swiftness of death. Whether Jack was killed instantly is therefore questionable. There was a tendency among fellow soldiers and officers, when writing to the relatives of the fallen, to explain the circumstances of death in a manner that made it sound cleaner and more palatable than the truth. This is understandable and we can only hope that there was no need for embellishment in Jack's case.

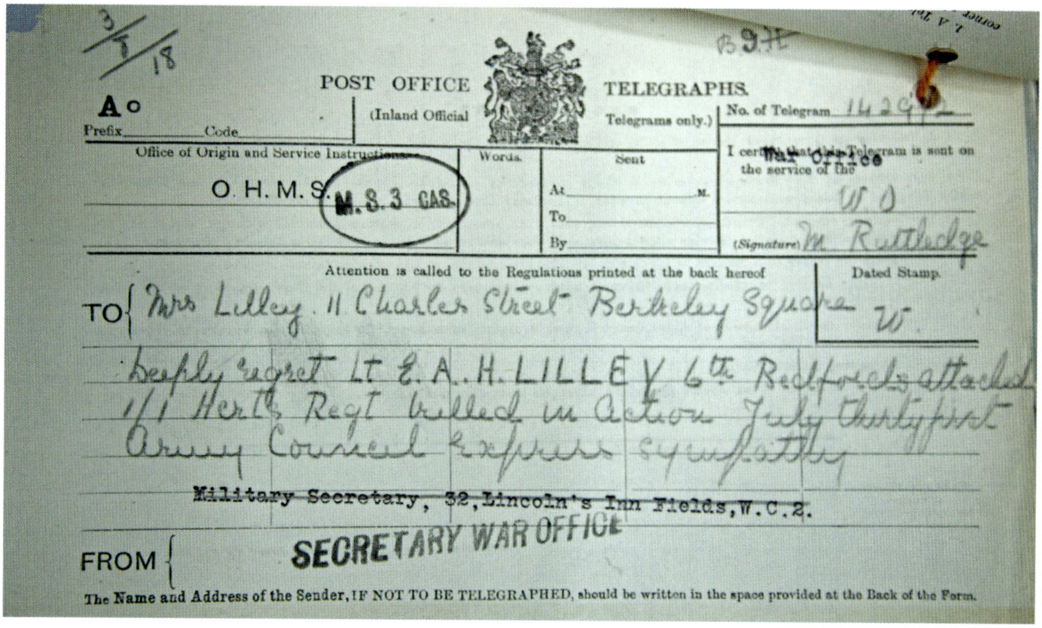
3/8/18

POST OFFICE TELEGRAPHS.
(Inland Official Telegrams only.)

Ao
Prefix Code

No. of Telegram 14297

Office of Origin and Service Instructions
O. H. M. S. M.S. 3 CAS.

Words Sent
At M.
To
By

I certify that this Telegram is sent on the service of the War Office
W.O.
(Signature) M Rutledge

Attention is called to the Regulations printed at the back hereof

Dated Stamp.

TO { Mrs Lilley. 11 Charles Street Berkeley Square W.

Deeply regret Lt E. A. H. LILLEY 6th Bedfords attached 1/1 Herts Regt killed in action July thirtyfirst Army Council express sympathy

Military Secretary, 32, Lincoln's Inn Fields, W.C.2.

FROM { SECRETARY WAR OFFICE

The Name and Address of the Sender, IF NOT TO BE TELEGRAPHED, should be written in the space provided at the Back of the Form.

The War Office telegram sent to Jack's wife Annie dated 3 August 1918.

Since Jack was an officer a telegram reached his wife Annie within four days of his death. The families of other ranks were informed by conventional post which would take a little longer. Notification could exceed two weeks if the soldier's death occurred during a major offensive. Naturally relatives would want as much detail as possible about what happened as well as the location of the grave. In Jack's case eye-witness accounts were received and his body removed to a cemetery without delay.

Ivan doesn't give us much sense of how it felt to lose his cousin, who became yet another wooden cross to be photographed on behalf of a grieving wife or mother. In his diary he laconically notes 'Hear of poor Jack's death.' Perhaps he was more emotive in letters that haven't survived. Jack does, however, feature heavily in the diaries of Ivan's sister Viola. She evidently held a deep affection for Jack and her diaries imply she had romantic feelings for him. She expresses a profound sense of loss and grief in her diary from 1918:

> On August 4th, the anniversary of the war and a day of intercession, I returned from the Downs with Lorna [her dog] before breakfast. I had picked some hare bells. Father came out to the back door and called me and wonderingly I answered him. He said nervously, 'Viola, there's very bad news from Jack.' As he paused I said 'Yes?' thinking if the news came from Jack he was just wounded or ill. Father continued, 'As you might have expected (he tells me now he first said in his nervousness "As you might have hoped") he's been killed, leading a Trench Mortar Battery.' In an indifferent sort of voice, as if listening to uninteresting news I said 'Oh', and father added the remark that Aunt Millie was upstairs in hysterics, and then he went back to the dining room. Mechanically I put the hare bells in water, fetched my breakfast in, pushed it down somehow in a sort of feverish haste to get away, and then went on with my normal duties. All through the morning I carried on with work in the same stunned sort of way, not allowing myself to think, and perfectly dry eyed. As I was peeling potatoes Aunt Polly came up to me and whimperingly said something about, 'Isn't it awful about poor Jack!' and some other words about me always being good to him. I answered in the same indifferent tone. I forget if she kissed me. Sylvia and father went to church. I went and picked all the violas, a job I'd been meaning to do for some days and as I carried a bowlful into the breakfast room mother came down and followed me in and kissed me without saying a word. That was better and made my eyes just moisten. She also went to church. Later, Aunt Millie came out into the kitchen with her cup and saucer, her face swollen with crying. I was grinding salt for the saltcellar. She cried sobbingly to me, 'Oh Viola, what are we going to do!' I quickly

left the salt, put my arm round her neck and kissed her again and again, but said no word. She went away weeping, and just for a moment my own tears fell.

I took some pure white violas up to Vailima [her garden grotto] and put them before his photo. I forgot how the afternoon passed, but I managed to read to father just before tea. After tea I copied out the Brig. General's letter telling the news and wrote to him asking to explain why Jack had to be transferred to another Battalion and why he thought himself a failure. I also wrote to Eva. I read some of his latest letters, and at last I wept. And every day since tears have come more and more frequently, some thoughts torment me, thoughts of the past, and dull, aching misery when I think of different things I was to show him and tell him of.

I walked down to church this morning alone with father and was somewhat cheered by his belief that the dead are not sleeping but are quite near us. But the change is what worries me. If he is near me and yet a sort of glorified being and not the dear faulty boyish boy that I love so much it can be no comfort to have him near. More hopeful views may come later.

I see Tennyson says:

'Those we love first are taken first. God gives us love. Something to love He lends us; but, when love is grown to ripeness, that on which it throve falls off, and love is left alone.'

August 5 Jack, I can't bear it!

August 6 Beautiful letter from his friend to Aunt Millie, telling of his splendid death. Copied it out. Cried a lot.

August 7 Feel worse than ever, and can't stop crying at certain thoughts. Put all his letters together in a wooden box and started painting it mauve.

Jack's dog tag. I found this tucked inside one of Viola's diaries that had originally belonged to Jack's mother (Aunt Millie), with the words 'Melina Elizabeth Lilley, Jan 27 1879, Strictly Private' written in the front. It was barely used by her, evidently bequeathed to Viola around 1934.

August 8 Another weary, aching tearful day. Lorna went away in night and hasn't come back, and her puppies are due!

August 11 Took Father to church. Was able to talk of things a bit and gained some comfort.

August 16 Felt better at first, but a few of Jack's things arrived by second post, and I'm down again. Gave Aunt Polly a summer birthday and tea in the garden.

August 18 I am beginning to find myself again, and God, and Jack. Today I got nearer to reality. It is windy and sunny and I went out on the Downs before breakfast and the veil between us was very thin indeed. Every time I get this intense enjoyment of nature I know I am half in that other land. But at home there are constant reminders by post of the earthly side of death, and until such reminders cease I cannot entirely realise the joy and beauty of it all. His fountain pen, wrist watch, pocket book, cigarette case arrived a few days ago, together with a sketch in black and white paint of the grave, done by one of the men. I had hoped never to see a picture of his grave. I don't want it! And all his things are to arrive soon. Until that is all over there cannot be real peace. The box with all his letters in it and with photos and things on top is the shrine of the only love I ever had. I do not wear mourning for him but I wear a dress to do him honour. White dress, white hat with amethyst band round it, amethyst and white silk sash, white shoes and stockings, and a few amethyst coloured violas at my neck. I know he would have loved the effect.

The Brig. General has written a nice letter explaining everything and saying that as Jack was so run down he was about to be given six months leave! Oh, why need I have been told that!

August 25 Spent evening in Vailima, reading his letters, Tennyson, and Wordsworth. Broke down over one of the letters. Miss him, and need him more than ever.

August 27 The G.R. people wrote to say Jack is buried in St Amand Cemetery, near Doullens.

The letter from the DGR&E referred to by Viola was written on 14 August from the London office and states:

Viola Bawtree with her dog Lorna in 1917.

> Madam, I am directed to inform you that a report has been received which states that Lieutenant E.A.H. Lilley, 6/Bedfordshire Regiment attd 1/1st Hertfordshire Regt. is buried in St Amand British Cemetery, South West of Arras. The grave has been registered in this office, and is marked by a durable wooden cross with an inscription bearing full particulars.

This letter was typical of many that might arrive following the death of a soldier. Other notifications would inevitably follow regarding issues such as personal effects, the deceased's will, pensions and, if requested, the photographs that Ivan and his colleagues were producing.

September 26 Jack's effects arrived at last.

November 3 Shall I ever realise he is with me? Even belief is sometimes shaken about it. Oh, if only Christ could have told us something about it all, so that I could have ground for belief. If he is not with me now, we are going to lose our personality, for so long as he remained himself he couldn't help staying with me.

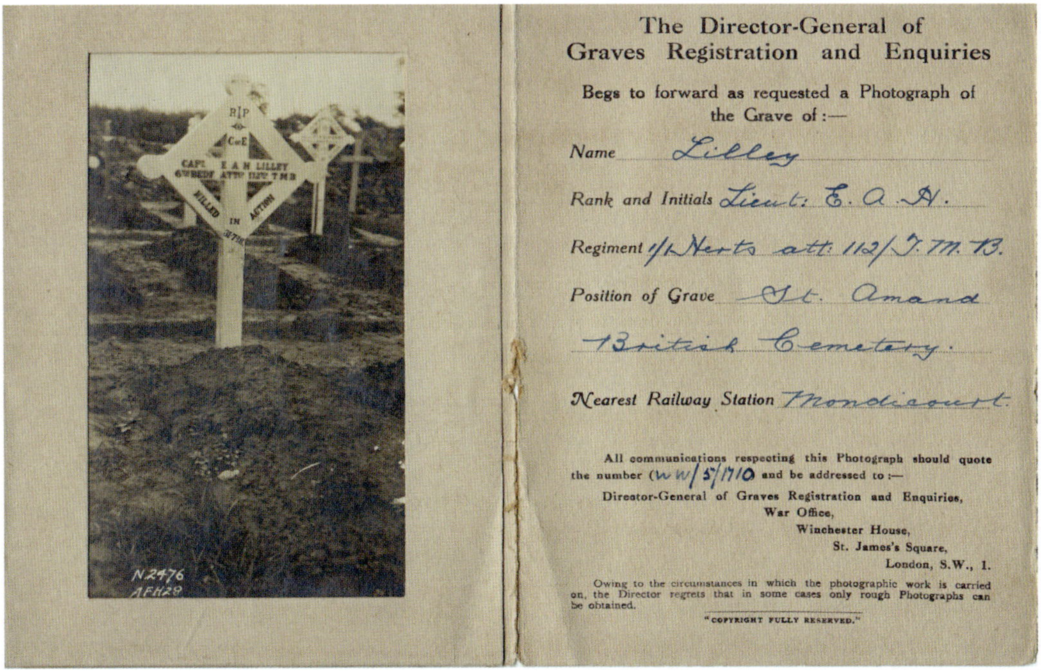

This photo of Jack's grave is typical of what was sent to the next of kin. It informed them of where their relative was buried and the nearest railway station.

> **November 10** He is with me. I know it. One day I shall realise his presence. We are still together, sharing everything. The hellish nightmare of war is nearly over. He is as intensely interested as I am, and is seeing the result of all he suffered and fought for. The world is waiting now for Germany to agree to the Allies' terms and sign the armistice. Then – Peace!
>
> I often wondered how it would begin to come and felt I should not be able to bear the gladness of it. But it's coming grandly, solemnly. The thought of all that has happened to bring it about and of all who have died; the thought of the terrible epidemic of influenza now still raging everywhere and killing fresh ones everyday; and the thought of the chaos and suffering in enemy countries. All these things sober us and we just wait for the angel of peace, who is so very near now, with a sort of hushed and reverent awe, mixed with intense, overwhelming relief. And the whole world has been brought nearer to the Kingdom of Heaven!

I suspect Viola's expression of grief epitomized what so many were going through across the land, indeed in every land embroiled in this war. While receiving a drawing of Jack's grave was distressing for her as it shattered any illusion that he might still be alive, so many were left with the agonizing situation of only knowing that their loved one was 'missing'. While this offered a thin line of hope that the missing soldier might be recovering in a hospital somewhere or a prisoner of war, in the vast majority of cases it simply meant that they had vanished on the battlefield, lost in muddy quagmires or blown to pieces, never to be seen again. Consequently, they would have no known grave. A lack of hard evidence of the death of a soldier would effectively put the grief process on hold, leaving the relatives with a deep need to piece together what might have happened. Viola, though at first inconsolable, at least had plenty of information from the DGR&E and from Jack's comrades who were with him when he fell.

Jack's grave in St Amand British Cemetery.

When peace was signed at Versailles in June 1919, Viola wrote the following powerful sentiments:

St Amand British Cemetery: a beautiful and serene place.

June 28 Peace to be signed at 3pm today. Later, maroons, guns, ad lib. during evening. Silly rot! What is there to rejoice about with all the fearful trouble in Germany? The time to rejoice was when the guns stopped killing.

June 29 Yesterday, the Germans signed the Peace Treaty: Peace was signed, and I could not rejoice. Germany has been humiliated to the dust, her country is in a seething, chaotic, turbulent condition.

What then are we to rejoice about? The real rejoicing came last Nov.11th when at last the guns ceased firing and the hideous massacre ceased. Then was the time to rejoice.

Peace celebrations now seem to me a silly farce. To say Germany has deserved all her trouble etc. etc., is nothing to do with it. I cannot feel we should rejoice. At dusk yesterday the fireworks started. I stood and watched them all round the horizon and first felt only like crying. But when I realized it was after all an historic night and that all over the world the same sort of thing was going on, I became fascinated and could not tear myself away. There was no cause to rejoice but I liked to feel it was a great day in history and that all the world was taking part. And I knew there were all 'Those Others' too, looking on those who had

> fought and died for it, and that they saw deeper than we did and knew really that they had not died in vain. All the frivolity and silliness is probably only reaction, but what a much nobler, finer England it seemed while the war was on. Do we already need another big trial to call out the good in us, or will it gradually assert itself as the world settles down a bit? And why does no one ever sympathise with Germany? Plenty of pity perhaps, magnanimous pity, but I come across no sympathy at all. Bad look out for us all if God were so unsympathetic!

The Cenotaph in Westminster on 12 November 2015.

On 18 November 1919 she wrote:

> Went to London to meet Mr & Mrs & Hilda Lawrence. Like them very much, especially Mrs. She and I walked together and talked of her boy, and of Jack. We had our first sight of the Cenotaph, and Mrs L cried. [Mr and Mrs Lawrence's son was one of Jack's pals killed around June 1918.]

The Cenotaph, designed by Sir Edwin Lutyens, was originally made of wood and plaster to be part of the London Victory Parade in June 1919. It provided a much-needed focus for national grief and consequently it was decided to create a permanent stone structure that was finally unveiled by King George V on Armistice Day 1920.

Chapter Seven

The War Ends, the Work Continues

The War Draws to an End

By August 1918 the tide of the war had inexorably turned in favour of the allies, culminating in the armistice signed on 11 November. Ivan commented on the war as it entered its final stages and life was attempting to get back to 'normal'.

Clearing the ground at Hooge Crater Cemetery, 3 miles east of Ypres.

These paragraphs are taken from a letter he wrote to Viola dated 16 October 1918:

> There is a lot of peace talk in the air but everything seems in a great muddle. I can't understand the situation. One thing is certain is that the Germans are getting thoroughly beaten everywhere. We are expecting to hear good news from our part of the world. You will have already read it in the papers but we haven't seen the papers yet.
>
> **17/10/18** We have seen some of the news in the French paper. Things are going very well. The trees are looking very autumnal now. I like this time of the year the best. However bright the sun may appear in the autumn the light is not so good as the summer or spring light, but it is splendid weather for making photographic pictures. The mist in the atmosphere makes everything in a landscape soften down, and only the subject near the camera comes out really distinct.
>
> We have had a great deal of wet weather this week and the roads are in a shocking condition for cycling. On Monday I cycled to one of the cemeteries where everything has got overgrown with grass because it was dangerous to work there until recently [Ivan's diary shows this was at Brandhoek which lies between Ypres and Poperinghe]. The Germans are far away from there now. I spent four hours there cutting the grass on the graves I had to photograph and took 70 photos. It was very stiff work. I came back late in the afternoon through the town we were staying at from Christmas to March [Poperinghe] and I could easily imagine I was going home to the billet there for things are almost normal again apart from the ruined buildings. I met the usual stream of Chinese carrying loads of fresh vegetables and singing in the weird way that only they know how to sing. In the town there seemed the usual bustle and the people were just beginning to put up the shutters of the shops.

Long-Awaited Leave

At this point Ivan had not been home on leave since June 1917. Getting back to England was still not a possibility so he applied for leave in France. He writes: 'It was announced that British soldiers who had been without leave for over 12 months could have one on the continent. So Athel and I were able to organise a leave to Brittany to which we travelled by train from Boulogne to Paris and then to Guingamp and Paimpol.'

In a letter to his mother dated 27 October 1918, he details the leave he managed to arrange with Athel that began with a somewhat arduous journey and some interesting sights:

> The 22nd was a dull, damp day. I went out on the bicycle to several places. In the evening I got my leave pay at our DAD town and discovered that they were moving up up up, oh I don't know how far forward and yet they were going to a back area! My letters can still be addressed the same. [The 'DAD town' was in Wormhoudt in France and moved east to Roubaix at this time.]
>
> That evening the son of the woman at the bread shop arrived home on leave and I had to spend the night at the camp because he had to use the spare bed. I had a bath and got everything packed up. In the morning I strapped the kit on the bicycle and at 10am I set off after depositing all remaining kit and all my office stuff at the town mayor's office. That same day Unit No. 3 moved to the ruined place already mentioned [Ypres]. When I go back I shall probably find my kit with Unit No. 4 where I expect to work in future. (-6.30pm. Time for dinner eh what?) At any rate I shan't be living at the same place, worse luck. I was very comfortable there.
>
> Now I will say a few words about bicycles. The machine I have to work on is a £3.10 Gamage machine which is a terror. Ever since I have had it, it has kept falling to pieces. The freewheel particularly has always been jibbing. Last week it absolutely gave up the ghost. Now in order for my leave to correspond with Athel's it was necessary to go down to Boulogne by bicycle and as the Gamage was the only machine available I had to set to and repair it myself.
>
> It was thoroughly worn out and most of the ball bearings had disappeared. I had to make two new pauls or little half-moon of metal which engage in the cog wheel when you push the pedals. I succeeded in making these but had no means of hardening the iron. All the same I hoped that even the soft iron would carry me as far as Boulogne. I gave the machine a complete week's rest and good supply of oil and hoped for the best. You will have noticed by my card what became of the venture. It was the toughest journey I have ever made in my life. I went 10 kilometres in fine style and then the blessed freewheel began to give out and after another ten kilometres it fell to pieces and all its inside fell out. Very cheerful as I had 50 more kilometres yet to go. First thing I did was to have some eggs and chips. Then I went to a cycle shop (I happened to have reached a large town) and asked if they could do anything but they were hopeless. Then I turned the machine upside down and had the wheel to pieces. With the help of a butcher's

boy who nobly came to my assistance we crammed a couple of old nails into the wheel in the hopes of getting the wheel to catch. It did catch for two kilometres but then again you could pedal 100 miles an hour without moving an inch. I visited the village blacksmith and again had the thing to pieces. We crammed a couple of large horseshoe nail-heads into the thing and screwed it up tight. This repair lasted me about 10 or 15 kilometres then the thing again went squiffy at a place where there wasn't any blacksmith. I had to take it to pieces and turn the bits of iron so that they gripped again. Then I started off again. I met with more terrible hills than I have met before. One hill was as steep as Reigate Hill only more than six times the length. For the next 20 kilos I had to walk the greater part of the way. Sunset found me on the top of the hills slowly making my way along the lonely road. I managed to push on until I was 13 kilos from Boulogne and then my worst fears were realised and the wheel gave out. Then I started on a long 8-mile tramp (mostly uphill) to Boulogne. The road was very lonely and very dark as I had to pass through a big forest. At last I reached the outskirts of Boulogne and was soon at Athel's place. I got there at 8.30pm. He gave me a good supper and I spent the night in the Sgt's room. The following day I did some shopping and had a look round the town. I enjoyed it very much as it is a long time since I have visited the place. I slept the night at the same place. The following morning we left Boulogne by the 11 o'clock train and had a very comfortable journey to Paris. En route we passed a large place which the Germans tried so hard to get and nearly succeeded [this was Amiens]. They have not improved the appearance of the place nor of the surrounding country.

We got to Paris at 4.30. All we saw of it was just like London. We had a military bus as far as the Gare St Lazare but found that that was the wrong station so we went underground. I was very favourably impressed by the underground. Everything was very clear to find your way and both trains and tubes were well lit. They were

A ruined shop in Amiens.

very smart in getting the trains off too. We went to the Gare de Montparnasse and after considerable delay obtained tickets for Paimpol.

Then we tried to get something to eat. We found a small restaurant but had to puzzle a lot over the names of things. Athel ordered an hors d'oeuvres instead of poissons. Athel's appetite and tastes are still just extraordinary. I had most of his share of raw herrings and underdone beef. Cela ne fait rien. I am making the best of things in the mangé line. We tried to see Paris but it was much too dark. The artificial illumination in the Place de La Concorde was quite brilliant. We were able to see the thousands of German guns which are ranged all around the big square. We also saw a German tank and several aeroplanes. We saw the statue to the town of Lille with all the wreaths in front of it. Our train left at 8.08 pm. It was not very comfortable and was full up with French soldiers mostly. We arrived at the junction at Guingamp at 6.30 in the morning. I have sent a lot of views of the place which is very picturesque and ancient. We had a very interesting walk through the streets. It was a new land to us. The national head dress is a peculiar affair of white lace which Athel has no doubt described. The girls are all very pretty with large eyes. The eyes of both boys and girls are the striking feature of the Breton. We had a glumpshous breakfast at a little restaurant in the Grande Place. A large cup of coffee with cream and plenty of bread and beautiful fresh butter, but my! didn't it cost a lot. We caught the narrow gauge train at 9.30 and got to Paimpol at midday. Here we found a large crowd waiting not for our benefit, but because they expected some German prisoners to arrive. We were met by a very nice man, a sailor by profession but he has been in the trenches and had his leg wounded. Now he is discharged and is the fiancé of our host's daughter. He conducted us to the house which is a fashionable nice house on the quayside at Paimpol... We were made very welcome at the house which is quite imposing and well fitted inside. We were shown our rooms – very nice ones with electric light and everything you could want. Athel's room is like a state bedroom with the bed recessed and another little recess for the washing room. Both rooms look out over the harbour. After a wash we went down to lunch. I may say that the meals are absolutely great after what I have been used to at the camp. Eight or nine course for lunch and ditto for dinner. There are one or two surprise packets but we got on very well. They give you vin rouge and cider to drink. Athel is very amusing with his grub especially when he suspects (1) that a thing is only partially cooked or (2) that it has pork in it. Last night for instance (at 6.30pm) we had soup first then sausages and potatoes, then a beautiful piece of cold bacon. Then roast mutton and tomato sauce with salad etc. Then some rice pudding, then cheese, then nuts and apples followed by coffee. At lunch we had roast pork as one of the items. Athel would not touch it of course. The other day we had raw oysters of all things with lemon juice and bread and butter. Athel ate two! He considers himself now one of the greatest heroes that ever lived. I had a lot because I found they were quite tasteless and it was a good excuse for eating some nice bread and fresh butter.

The chap that met us at the station then took us for a stroll around the town. It is quite a large fishing town about the same size as Lyme Regis... We went to the Gendarmerie where the Sgt. Major signed our passes. We visited the church which is new and yet quite presentable... The following morning we had our petit dejeuner at 8.30, coffee and bread and butter – tres bon. He asked us if we'd like to go to Mass at the church but I didn't fancy it. Then he suggested us going to the protestant service. It appears that an English missionary has been here for 16 years and has quite a fair following. We went to the house but found that he was ill and suspected that he was going to have influenza, so we fixed up to call on Monday afternoon and went for a walk to Kerity instead of going to church [an influenza epidemic had swept across Europe at the time and would prove more deadly even than the war]. We met an English sailor (there are several of them about as there are four English vessels in the port) and had an interesting conversation with him. He said he had never seen any English about in these parts before. Then we walked on picking blackberries off the hedges en route... We met a couple of the natives who thought they recognized me as a chap they had met when prisoners of war in Germany. They had been repatriated. They asked me if I had ever been a prisoner.

In the afternoon the chap who had met us at the station and Miss Bonne and the little kids and the little dog all came with us for a walk to the nearest point where you can look over the sea.

After dinner we went into the drawing room and had a bit of a sing-song. Athel played the usual selection on the piano and sang the Marseillaise for them and Miss Bonne also gave us a song. Then Athel and I sang Tipperary ha! ha! Yesterday we had a very jolly day...

Ivan's leave with Athel would last until 1 November when he had to wend his way back on the train to Boulogne via Paris. He then managed to get a ride in a Ford car to St Omer and from there cycled to his billet at Unit 4, based in Abeele on the Franco-Belgian border. A few days later he would move once again to the familiar town of Poperinghe. He would not be granted leave to go home until the end of the following January.

The Armistice

> On November 10th at midnight all the railway engines on the light railways started whistling. On the morning of 11th November we heard that an armistice was to be signed at 11am as the Germans had surrendered. The troops went wild and fired Very lights and generally celebrated. A wonderful experience.

Ivan's 1918 diary is somewhat scant for such a momentous occasion. Here are the November entries around the armistice:

> **10.11.18** Pack up and move to Poperinghe. Fix up bed at new billet. Service at Talbot House and game of chess. Exciting night.

> **11.11.18** Armistice signed. Wet day. Fix up new office and clerical work. Write letters at billet in the evening.

> **12.11.18** Fine sunny weather. Cycle to Ebblinghem via Cassel. All the streets very gay with flags. Take 118. Hear terms of Armistice in evening. Clerical work and letter writing.

Graves Registration Unit Section No. 3 in Ypres.

13.11.18 Splendid news in the paper. [Ivan's copy of the *Daily Express* on this day still survives in fragile condition, with the headline 'The Terms of the Armistice'.] Fine, frosty morning. Cycle to Belgian Battery Corner via Divisional Cemetery. Then visit No.3 Unit at Ypres. Return via Hagle-Dump and Gwalia Farm. Clerical work until 10 pm.

14.11.18 Fine, and frosty weather. Cycle to Dozinghem, Mendinghem and Haringhe. Take 110. Clerical work until 9 pm. Good singsong in the square by moonlight.

Athel, who was based in Boulogne at the time, wrote the following in a letter to sister Sylvia dated 12 November 1918:

At last I can collect my thoughts to write to you. What with waiting day after day for the end, and then the excitement when the terms were actually signed, we seemed to have passed from death to a new life and everything has a different aspect. I actually had a kindly word to say of the moon this evening. I never thought I could do that again [bright moon = air-raids].

When the news came to us as [in the] enclosed paper – which please keep carefully as a souvenir, and it gradually dawned on people in its full significance, people went mad almost. All the sirens in the harbour sounded for hours at full blast, and guns went off from the ships there. Flags appeared like magic everywhere. Hosts of children paraded the streets singing the Marseillaise, and our own troops singing Rule Britannia. Oh my word! I can no more describe that day and its sensations and doings than I could the scenery in Brittany. I must give it up and leave you to fill in the blanks.

Thanks for your two letters and good wishes, and the yarns and also for the excellent chocolates which I much enjoyed. Please thank Aunt Milly very much for the soap which is very acceptable indeed and quite unprocurable here.

Your other letter was a sad one and also frightened me somewhat about the health of the family. I do hope you all avoid close atmospheres as much as you can. I doubt if it is wise for Ma and Dad to go to church until this recent news has so raised Public Health as to reduce the influenza.

I have heard from Ivan again today. He is back at Pop once more but a very different place from what it was, I thank God for that.

Love to all from Athel

Back in Sutton on 11 November, Viola wrote in her diary: 'The Great Day. At 11am all the guns and hooters went. We stood about listening. Mother cried. I nearly did. Then I dashed to Sutton, letting all the work go, Sylvia went on her bike. Flags and people happy faces everywhere. Drizzle began at 12.30.'

On 12 December 1918, Ivan wrote to Viola:

> It is a beastly wet day today – much too wet to go out to work. I have just heard that my motor-bicycle is to arrive today. I shall be very glad to get it.
>
> On Monday I went to Ypres and nearly to Zonnebeke on the bicycle. On my return through Ypres I took a photo of a Belgian dog-cart in front of the Cloth Hall. I enclose a copy. It is disappointing in some respects: (1) My idea was to get a Flemish picture i.e. just the dog-cart and the Cloth Hall but the Tommies would get in the picture (2) I took it a little bit too small (3) It is not well composed.

British soldiers pose with Belgian refugees and their dog-cart outside the Cloth Hall. These are likely some of the first former inhabitants to return to their town.

However, I have already sold 16 prints at 5d each and expect to sell several dozen. I have a jolly fine dark-room in the cellar here. Tuesday I went for a long cycle ride to Bergues as I had some photos to take in the cemetery there. It rained nearly all the time and roads were in a shocking bad state. I managed to buy some photographic paper and developer. To give you an instance that I meant what I said in Elaine's letter I bought the things on Tuesday and by Wednesday evening had paid myself for the materials out of the sale of prints and had some profit too. In the evening we had a good game of whist in the billet. Wednesday was a thoroughly wet day.

I spent the morning doing clerical work in the office and the afternoon in doing some prints of the Ypres view. Today also is pouring wet. I am sending in this letter a very interesting view of the Kaiser opening a German cemetery at St Quentin. It is a very good souvenir so please take care of it. I got it from Cpl Haddon who got it from a German prisoner.

I also enclose a view of Bedford House Cemetery south of Ypres on the canal bank. It has been very badly shelled and this photo which I took was not passed

The view of Kaiser Wilhelm inaugurating the German Military Cemetery at St Quentin on 18 October 1915.

because it looked too rough to send to the relatives. This is not my opinion. I think a soldier's grave should be on the battlefield and personally should appreciate such a photo. What do you think?

It is not far off Christmas now is it? I have no chance of leave yet a while.

Most of the men who have come from Sutton were in the meadow and remember Clapham Lodge very well. Strange isn't it. [The meadow near Ivan's home was commandeered in March 1918 and used as a military camp.]

Hasn't Aunt Milley received a photo of Jack's grave yet? Perhaps I shall hear from you by today's mail and in case the mail doesn't go til tomorrow morning so I will add to this letter if there is anything to put bye and bye.

No letter today.

The motor-bicycle arrived this afternoon but unfortunately they have sent a chauffeur with it. He will be in the way. Well, cheerio.

Once the war was over there was still plenty of work for Ivan to do in terms of registering and photographing graves. It must have felt never-ending. The year 1918 saw victory but had yielded a vast harvest of casualties just like its predecessors. The military situation had also severely hindered the work of the DGR&E, with many forward areas becoming inaccessible, thus creating a large backlog.

The armistice freed up previously unreachable areas for Ivan and his colleagues to register and photograph graves. The danger of shellfire and shrapnel was now over but Ivan still had to navigate through devastated terrain replete with ruins, waterlogged and damaged roads, thick mud, unexploded ordnance and other war-related debris.

In addition to his usual work Ivan documented two of the most important jobs that had to be carried out after the war had ended. Firstly, it was necessary to comb the battlefields for isolated graves and the remains of the missing and then arrange for their subsequent removal and reburial in a military cemetery. Secondly, the makeshift cemeteries that had all sprung up interwoven with the battle-scarred landscape needed to be cleared up to pave the way for their transformation into permanent spaces of remembrance.

Recovery and Reburial of the Missing

Hundreds of thousands of British and Commonwealth soldiers were missing in action, presumed lost in the battlefield chaos and quagmires. It was the job of the Graves Concentration Units, made up of the GRUs, Labour Companies and other units, to carry out the hazardous and gruesome task of combing the battlefields in search

Parties searching for bodies.

of remains. Ivan documented the work of one such unit, the 129 Labour Company, on the Passchendaele battlefield in the Ypres Salient, shown in the following set of photographs. The commentaries on each picture come from Captain G. Crawford of the 68 Labour Company who formulated some instructions that became the standard procedure for the Graves Concentration Units.

> Each squad [of 32 men] should be given an area consisting of a map square of 500 yards, which must be thoroughly searched and cleared…advantage should be taken of natural features where possible, as it is much easier to search the area, say, between a road and a trench, or a line of pill boxes, than to work upon imaginary lines between flags…the men, should be posted in extended order at intervals of about six yards. They must advance slowly, searching the area thoroughly, and avoid bunching. Wherever a body is found, a stake is to be planted…
>
> Experience only teaches men where bodies will probably be found in graves which are not visible, but the following signs are characteristic…rifles or posts bearing helmets or equipment, placed at the head of graves…remains or

A body found. A tin helmet can be seen on the ground.

equipment upon the surface or protruding from the ground…rat holes – these sometimes will show small bones or pieces of equipment brought to the surface by the rats…discolouration of grass, earth or water – grass is often of a vivid bluish green colour where bodies are buried and water turns a greenish black or grey… The area having been thoroughly searched and staked out, the work of exhumation begins.

Each party of four should have with them shovels, rubber gloves, canvas and rope, Cresol [disinfectant] and stretchers…at the present time, conditions are against rapid work: the battlefields are covered with a growth of rank grass and nettles, in places almost waist high, which often conceals the more obscure traces by which bodies can be discovered…an area must be swept and re-swept before it is definitely decided that no graves have been overlooked. This is especially important because after an area has been described as clear, any graves registered in that area which have not been found [must] definitely be regarded as lost.

In the actual work of exhumation the men should be warned not to dig too closely to the bodies, but well outside them. Such a precaution renders the work

Digging up remains from wet ground.

Remains awaiting removal to a cemetery.

easier, prevents disturbance of the bodies and, most important of all, reveals whether more than one man is buried in one particular spot…men engaged upon exhumation should be instructed to use Cresol generously, especially for washing their hands and their gloves after handling bodies or effects…during the summer, work should be in the early morning.

The body, having been exhumed, is placed upon the canvas and a careful search is made for any effects which may lead to identification. The pockets should be searched, and a special examination made of the neck, wrists and braces, where identity discs may be found.

All effects are placed in a ration bag and sent to the cemetery attached to the body. Where more than one body is found the remains must be kept and sent to the cemetery together, and the labels so marked that the cemetery officer will bury them side by side…it is often possible from records to identify unknowns from the fact that they are known to have been buried with the identified men.

Skeletal remains of an unknown soldier found with equipment including a rifle.

The remains are then wrapped in the canvas, which is tied up and labelled… It has been found useful to mark all labels of one group of bodies with a distinctive letter of the alphabet, followed by a number showing the order in which they are to be buried…a union flag should be provided for each wagon or ambulance to cover the bodies.

Pay book, purse and other articles likely to help establish the identity of the remains.

The work of transporting the bodies to the cemetery is usually carried out by GS [General Service] wagons. No other transport can be used over the rough tracks which often have to be traversed. Motor ambulances are used where parties are working near the main road, or to take the bodies from the wagons as soon as they reach the main road…each GS wagon can take five loaded stretchers, four on top and one in the bottom. A stretcher should be allotted to each body, except in the case of fragmentary remains.

A spare man from the Exhumation Company should be allotted to each GS wagon to see that required stores are taken up to the working parties. He should walk behind the wagon when it is loaded with bodies to see that no accident happens on the way to the cemetery.

The bodies being brought to the cemetery, all effects are examined carefully and compared with the labels attached. A magnifying glass should be used to read the discs…if any query arises as a result of the examination, the exhuming officer, whose signature will be on the label, can be questioned when he reports at the cemetery, as he should do each day.

The size of the digging party depends upon the number of bodies expected to be received at the cemetery each day…under ordinary conditions, ten to twelve men should be able to dig a trench sufficient to take twenty bodies, and to carry out the reburials during ordinary working hours. It is the sanitary man's duty to see that as soon as the bodies have been removed, the stretchers are washed in Cresol and returned to the wagons.

Bodies arriving at a cemetery by GS wagon for reburial.

Last Post at a reburial service at Passchendaele New Concentration Cemetery.

> The bodies are then placed in their respective positions and the graves filled in either with or without a committal service (this will depend on whether, in the opinion of the Officer present at the exhumation, the body has previously been properly committed or not)...stakes bearing labels giving particulars of the men buried beneath are then erected at the head of the graves...until the GRUs erect crosses.
>
> It has been found advisable to impress upon [the men] that the work is of vital importance, having regard to the number of men still missing, many of whom can be found and identified if the work is carefully done...the greater the stress laid upon the need for identification, the greater the interest the men take in the work.

It was a race against time to exhume bodies as identification would become more difficult as time went on. About 80 per cent of exhumations remained unidentified and would receive a headstone with Rudyard Kipling's epitaph 'A Soldier of the Great War, Known unto God'. By October 1921 all military staff involved in exhumations had been withdrawn, even though about 200 bodies were still being found per week at that point. Some 204,654 bodies had been exhumed and transferred to the concentration cemeteries, but about 300,000 were still missing.

Men at work in Passchendaele New Concentration Cemetery.

A huge stack of crosses awaits use in Ypres, most likely for the concentration cemeteries.

Farmers were given official notice that they must inform the civil authorities or the IWGC immediately in the event of discovering any soldier's remains. About another 40,000 bodies would be discovered by those working for the IWGC and others such as farmers up to 1937. Bodies have continued to be found (largely by farmers, construction workers and archaeologists) over the years up to the present day, with an estimated 165,000 still missing on the Western Front. Remains found now have a new possibility of identification via DNA samples.

Clearing the Cemeteries

The DGR&E personnel helped clear up the cemeteries, shifting dangerous debris such as barbed wire and shells, before handing them over to the civilian care of the Imperial War Graves Commission. Many cemeteries had been damaged by frequent shellfire. Scouring the battlefields and clearing up front-line cemeteries was a somewhat dangerous task as they were littered with unexploded ordnance. The war diary for the Canadian War Graves Detachment noted on 31 May 1919: 'All ranks were again warned as to the care to be taken with unexploded ammunition.' Just three days earlier the diary recorded that two men had been 'accidentally injured through a lorry going over a Mills Grenade which was half buried' in the Lens sector.

Men in Hooge Crater Cemetery clearing the ground of war relics such as barbed wire and putting in stakes for new fencing.

Clearing up some shells at Hooge Crater Cemetery.

Making ground ready, Passchendaele New Cemetery.

Bucquoy Road Cemetery, 11 miles to the south of Arras. The cemetery is being prepared to be handed over to the care of the IWGC.

IWGC gardeners planting shrubs at Lijssenthoek Nursery Garden.

Chapter Eight

The Imperial War Graves Commission

As the war progressed it became increasingly clear that an organization would need to be established that would undertake the task of acquiring and maintaining land in perpetuity in order to accommodate the burgeoning cemeteries along the Western Front and in many other theatres of war around the

IWGC Arras Area Headquarters.

This photo is simply captioned 'GRU Headquarters', yet it features some of the most important figures who helped forge the IWGC. The man standing in the middle is Fabian Ware. Front row men from left: Sir George Perley (Canada), Admiral Sir Edmund Poë, Sir Thomas Mackenzie (New Zealand).

globe. The grand task of designing and building the cemeteries and memorials, likened by Rudyard Kipling to the greatest architectural endeavour since the pharaohs, awaited the termination of hostilities.

Therefore, on 21 May 1917 the Imperial War Graves Commission was established by royal charter, with the Prince of Wales as president and Fabian Ware remaining at the helm. The formation of the Commission would ensure the organization and maintenance of the war graves around the world ad infinitum. By this point about 300,000 graves had been registered in France and Belgium.

Since the Directorate of Graves Registration and Enquiries was part of the army it would disappear from the battlefields as the army gradually withdrew its presence after the war. Once the search for missing bodies had been officially called off in October 1921 the Directorate effectively closed.

The issue of how to commemorate the dead was not straightforward for the Commission. In fact, it was a veritable battleground as numerous questions had to be debated. All and sundry were expressing their hopes and demands. Many wanted their loved ones repatriated and commemorated in their own manner, while others including Ivan believed that a soldier should be buried within close proximity to the battlefield where he fell. The Commission was viewed by many as autocratic and even tyrannical in its decisions to dictate where and how the fallen would be buried and how the gravestones and memorials would ultimately be forged. Many felt that the army had taken their loved one in life, why should they take them in death as well?

It was, however, never going to be a free-for-all and uniformity was central to Ware's vision to embody the unity and sacrifice of the Empire rather than concede to the various desires of grieving relatives across a traumatized nation. At an IWGC meeting in November 1917 Major General Macready had stated that 'In the erection of memorials on the graves there should be no distinction between officers and men.' Permitting the repatriation of soldiers' remains or the erection of individual memorials would have played into the social differences that were being eroded by the war as only wealthier families would have had the means to fund such endeavours.

In May 1915 Ware had made his thoughts on repatriation abundantly clear in a letter to Lord Robert Cecil of the British Red Cross, following the exhumation and repatriation of William Glynne Charles Gladstone MP's body (grandson of Prime Minister William Gladstone) to British soil:

> There is possible trouble ahead about some exhumations at Poperinghe. I entirely agree with your remark about Gladstone's body. Incidentally, the exhumation was carried out by British soldiers under fire. Fortunately nobody was hit. The impression created among the soldiers out here is to be regretted. The one point of view that seems to me to be often overlooked in this matter is that of the officers themselves, who in ninety-nine cases out of a hundred will tell you that if they are killed would wish to lie among their men. To return to Gladstone, the administrative difficulty is not by the fact that permission was granted in his case because he was a Lord-Lieutenant. I am talking seriously. I understand that this was the reason suggested to the Highest quarters, and permission is not going to be given there in any future case.

Ultimately the argument that the average soldier desired to be buried alongside his comrades close to where they served and died held the greatest sway and the Commission thus ploughed ahead with its plans.

After the war the Commission was faced with the question of how to commemorate those who had no known grave. In the end the vast lists of names would be inscribed on grand memorials to the missing, such as Thiepval on the Somme and the Menin Gate in Ypres.

Ivan was attached to the DGR&E and did not mention the IWGC in his diaries that survive, but we know he was tasked with documenting much of the Commission's work in the immediate aftermath of the war. Therefore, it is through his camera lens that we get a great insight into the early operations of the Commission.

The first main camp was located in Hesdin in France where it operated with somewhat limited staff. In May 1919 it moved to a much larger site at Longuenesse near St Omer where it remained until 1929. This extensive and multi-faceted camp was established within the eighteenth-century Château de la Tour and its grounds and is depicted in the following set of Ivan's photographs.

IWGC HQ offices.

Canadian Colonel H.T. Goodland, who was the IWGC Deputy Controller, and his staff.

The draughtsmen's office where plans were drawn up for constructing the permanent cemeteries.

The architects' office.

The Commission acquired use of a nearby garage and workshop and thus created its own motor transport depot with a fleet of lorries, cars and motorbikes. Good transport was paramount to enable the gardeners and other labourers to get to the numerous cemeteries in the district. Some gardeners would have to go on extended excursions of a week or so in order to work on cemeteries further afield.

Travelling gardeners' lorry. Large numbers of British ex-servicemen were recruited to tend graves around France and Belgium.

The dispatch riders.

The lorry park.

The light car park.

The workshop for car repairs.

The men's quarters.

The No. 4 Stationary Hospital which became part of the IWGC Main Camp at Longuenesse.

The canteen.

One of the hospital wards.

The hospital dispensary.

Transforming the Cemeteries

Initially soldiers' graves had been marked with wooden crosses. These were to be replaced by proper headstones made from Portland stone (limestone). The IWGC made some effort to offer the wooden crosses to the respective relatives of the fallen, as long as they took responsibility for shipping them home. Not many took up the offer and the vast majority were destroyed in situ. Today many of the surviving wooden crosses can be found in churches across the nation.

An original wooden cross with an imprinted metal strip stating 'Unknown British Soldier' is displayed on the wall of the chapel at Talbot House in Poperinghe.

Ivan documented the production of the new headstones by Messrs Arrowsmith of Stockwell, London.

Planing the stone.

Lifting stones to the engraving room.

Final shaping and smoothing of headstones.

Many had argued in favour of using a cross rather than a headstone, but the headstones proved themselves to be considerably more versatile. They allowed much more information to be engraved: name, rank and date of death alongside the regimental badge. The religious affiliation of the individual soldier varied across the Empire, so a headstone allowed for different symbols, such as the Star of David, to be engraved and not just the Christian cross. Relatives were also allowed to add a brief epitaph. The French, however, did opt for a cross and the limitations are apparent: they simply say the soldier's name, date of death and 'Mort pour la France'.

Chiselling the regimental badge onto the headstone was quite an art and could take a stone mason a whole week to complete. Since

Engraving a headstone for a Canadian soldier. The soldier's name had yet to be inscribed but zooming in to the bottom of the headstone shows the reference: P3 RA C20 DOULCCE. This translates to Plot 3, Row A, Column 20 of Doullens Communal Cemetery Extension. A search through CWGC records reveals the soldier's identity as Private John Weatherhead of the Canadian Army Medical Corps.

The Jewish Star of David of Private J.B. Wynne among all the Christian crosses in Lijssenthoek Military Cemetery.

several hundred thousand headstones were required this was far too slow, and so machines were developed to do the job much faster.

The Commission held to the following principles in respect of the headstones:

1. There should be no distinction made on account of military or civil rank, race or creed.
2. Each of the dead should be commemorated by name on a headstone or memorial.
3. Headstones and memorials should be permanent.
4. Headstones should be uniform.

Three experimental cemeteries were designed by Sir Reginald Blomfield and completed in 1920 in France: at Le Tréport on the coast, and Forceville and Louvencourt on the Somme. These proved triumphant in putting to rest the debate about repatriation, headstones and memorials.

An elevated view of Forceville Cemetery, Somme, looking towards Lutyens' Stone of Remembrance, April 1920.

A letter by the war poet Beatrix Brice, published in *The Times* on 2 September 1920, gave the new cemeteries a powerful endorsement, describing them with heartfelt approval and wonder:

> I write for those whose men, dead in battle, now rest there, where they gave their lives. I write for those who cannot go to France. Especially for those who for varying reasons opposed or were afraid of military cemeteries. I have just seen the finished work at Forceville, and it is the most perfect, the noblest, the most classically beautiful memorial that any loving heart or any proud nation could desire to their heroes fallen in a foreign land.

Le Tréport Military Cemetery, April 1920.

> Your own man has a wonderful grave, the nation has a wonderful monument.
>
> Think first of your idea of a cemetery. At best it is undistinguished; at the worst a confused and melancholy jumble. Think of a monument; you see an obelisk, a statue, some stone erection – there are many – and what special emotion do they rouse? You must read the inscription before you know whom or what they commemorate. But wherever the eye falls on one of these Acres of God men know at once, without question, that here soldiers of Britain laid down their lives.
>
> Picture this strangely stirring place. A lawn enclosed of close-clipped turf, banded across with line on line of flowers, and linked by these bands of flowers, uncrowded, at stately intervals, standing in soldierly ranks the white headstones. And while they form as perfect, as orderly a whole as any regiment on parade, yet they do not shoulder each other. Every one is set apart in flowers, every one casts its shade upon a gracious space of green. Each one, so stern in outline, is most rich in surface, for the crest of the regiment stands out with bold and arresting distinction above the strongly incised names.
>
> Beyond and behind them the stone of Remembrance – an Altar of Sacrifice – witnesses 'Their name liveth for evermore,' and through the midst a broad white pathway leads to the foot of the Cross, outstretched arms sheltering them and bearing the Sword.
>
> It is the simplest place, it is the grandest place I ever saw. It is filled with an atmosphere that leaves you very humble, that gives you wonderful thoughts.

It would take until 1938 for the Imperial War Graves Commission to complete all the cemeteries and memorials, the final unveiling being the Australian memorial at Villers-Bretonneux near Amiens. Then, just one year later, the Graves Registration Units would sadly be back in action as another war enveloped the globe.

Chapter Nine

Exploring the Western Front

Ivan's colleague Griffiths with the motorbike and sidecar, stuck in a waterlogged landscape in the Ypres Salient. The sign behind shows that they are in Wieltje on the north-east side of Ypres.

In the course of his everyday work Ivan was able to take numerous photographs of the ruins and devastation in northern France and Flanders. He captured the destruction wrought on many towns and villages as well as the battle-scarred landscape and relics of war. His photos are largely undated but it is likely that the vast majority were taken after the armistice when he would have been able to take photographs of whatever he pleased. This chapter is divided into two main regions that saw some of the most ferocious fighting for Commonwealth forces of the war: the Ypres Salient (the forward and back areas) in West Flanders, Belgium, and the Somme in Picardie, France. Ypres itself was the place most photographed by Ivan and so deserves its own chapter. I've included some of my own photographs to give a sense of how things look now and how the land still reveals evidence of the conflict. Aside from the numerous war cemeteries and memorials there are a number of preserved trenches, concrete bunkers, mine craters and areas of undulating shell-scarred ground still visible today.

The Ypres Salient

This zone includes some of the hardest-fought areas of the war for the British army on the Western Front. It was also the zone most explored by Ivan in the course of his work with the GRU. Ivan's photographs allow us to travel along the main arteries of the salient out of Ypres to the front line, as well as the back areas.

Even on a push bike he could access several places in the course of a day's work. On one day in March 1917 he covered 40 miles around the salient; a significant distance given the state of many of the roads at the time and the frequent threat of shellfire: 'Cycle to Ypres via Vlamertinghe. Go to Prison then Menin Gate and up to Menin Rd. South. Then back through square to Lille Gate. Shrapnel Corner to Ridgewood, Dickebusch, La Clytte, Reninghelst, 40 miles. Fine weather. New batch of requests in afternoon. Evening as usual.'

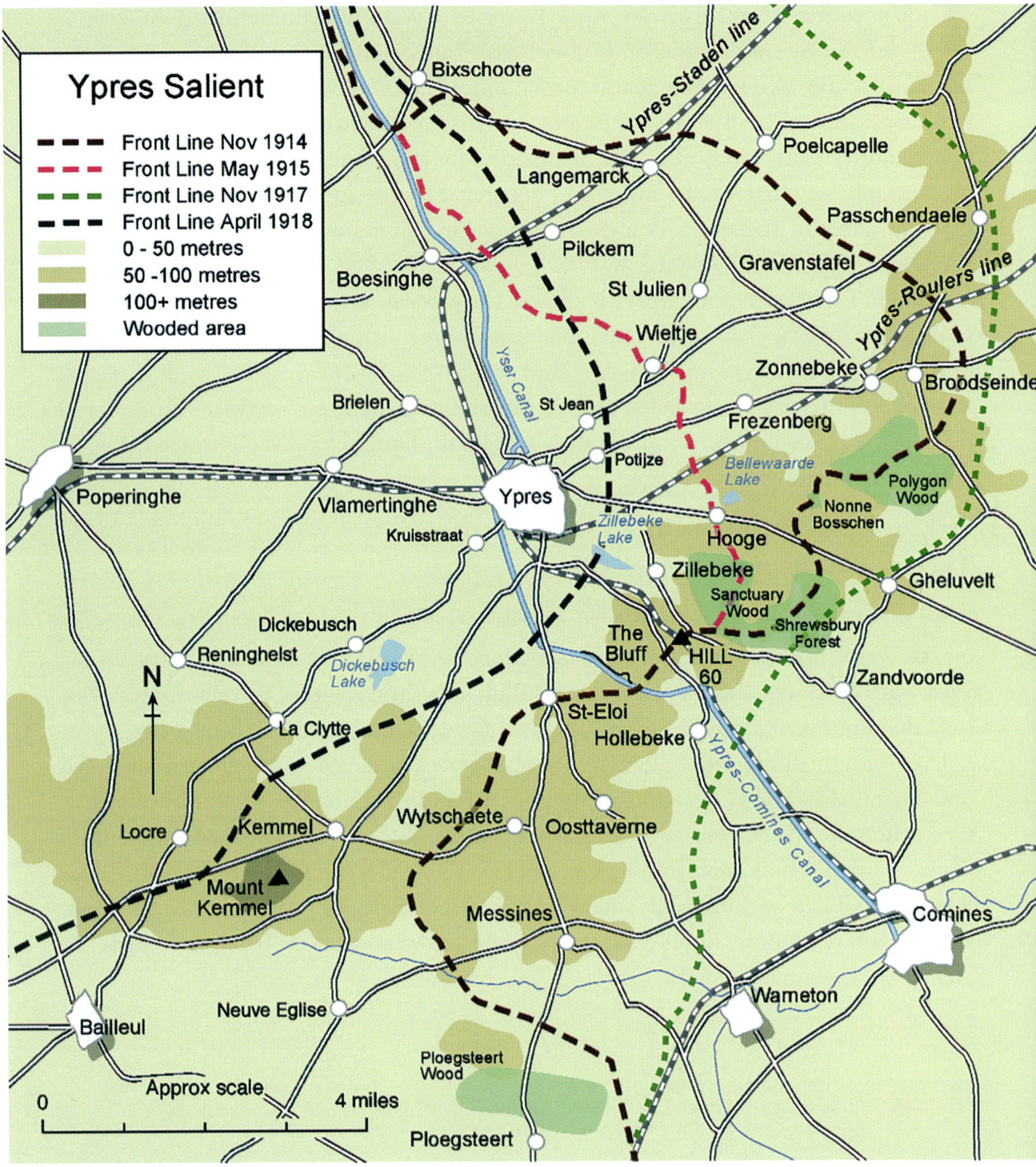

Map of the Ypres Salient showing many of the key areas where Ivan moved around. The position of the front line is shown at the conclusion of each of the major offensives that occurred in this sector.

Along the Menin Road

Ivan would often pass through the Menin Gate in Ypres and then turn right onto the Menin Road to visit Menin Road South Cemetery, then via 'Hellfire Corner' to Birr Cross Roads Cemetery and Hooge Crater Cemetery. In a letter to his mother dated 27 October 1918 he describes an excursion from Ypres to Gheluvelt, via the Menin Road. He provides a vivid description of the battlegrounds in this sector following the German retreat from the Ypres Salient:

> On the 21st I had a most interesting day. I went in the car to a famous ruined place and took some photos there. Then we found some jolly nice little dry dugouts where unit no. 3 is moving to (or rather it has moved by now). This place is now no longer a nasty place. It is far far from the war and out of range of shells for the first time since 1914. It was very interesting to visit it and find everything so quiet. Last time I was there in March when things were very lively. Then we went on in the car right up the main road through what was once the worst hell of the war. A veritable place of the dead. Nothing but a vast battleground with gaunt stumps of trees sticking up where woods had once been. One particularly famous spot was strewn with derelict tanks in all attitudes. Then we arrived at a part of the line which until last month had been held fast by the Germans. It was very interesting to see all his defences and dumps etc and guns which he had been unable to extricate during the hasty retreat. Any villages are mere names written on boards and the main road is about a foot deep in mud.

The tanks described by Ivan would most likely have been those of the 'Tank Graveyard' that was located just beyond Hooge near a crossroads known as 'Clapham Junction'. Some seventeen tanks were lost here during the opening phase of the Third Battle of Ypres in 1917.

The village of Hooge lay right in the midst of the fighting in the salient. Front-line trenches ran through it from May 1915 when the Germans pushed forward during the Second Battle of Ypres until the autumn of 1917 when they were pushed back again during the Third Battle of Ypres.

It is here that the most prominent remains of the war along the Menin Road can be found. In a wooded area on the north side of the road one can wander around German trenches and bunkers and a huge pond, created from three craters blown by German units in June 1916. Plenty of shell cases, barbed-wire stakes, elephant iron and other relics litter the ground.

Hellfire Corner on the Menin Road between Ypres and Hooge. During the war the British had screens up along the left-hand trees in the centre of this photograph to reduce visibility of the regular movements of troops and matériel. The Germans would frequently shell this area. Today it is a roundabout.

A desolate view of the Menin Road from Clapham Junction, between Hooge and Gheluvelt.

Entrance to a German bunker in Hooge.

Below: Devastation at Château Wood, Hooge. Duckboards had to be laid down amid the water-filled shell holes to have any hope of traversing this ground without being lost to the mud.

A German trench and barbed wire preserved at Hooge.

Shell cases litter the ground near the huge mine craters at Hooge, detonated by the Germans in 1916. Hooge Château, which was totally destroyed during the war, and Château Wood were located beyond this crater.

Hooge Village viewed from the cemetery. The dwellings are newly-built post-armistice as this place was reduced to nothing more than a 'mere name on a board'.

Just north of Clapham Junction on the Menin Road, heading towards Polygon Wood, is Glencorse Wood. Extensive fighting occurred around here as the First Battle of Ypres drew to a close and during the Third Battle.

An advanced dressing station at Glencorse Wood.

About 2 miles further along the Menin Road from Hooge is Gheluvelt. The allied advance during the Third Battle of Ypres reached Gheluvelt but failed to take this hard-fought-over village.

A view of Gheluvelt. The sign, clearly in readiness for gas attacks, reads: 'Alert Zone. Respirators will be worn – in alert position – forward of this point.'

The Road to Wieltje, St Julien and Poelcapelle

The road that leads out of the north-east corner of Ypres (the Brugeweg) takes you to Wieltje, St Julien and on to Poelcapelle. From here Ivan visited White House Cemetery (St Jean-les-Ypres), Oxford Road Cemetery, Wieltje Farm Cemetery, Seaforth Cemetery Cheddar Villa and Poelcapelle British Cemetery. Langemark and Cement House Cemetery can also be easily accessed from this road.

No photographs of the tank graveyard on the Menin Road feature in Ivan's collection; however, there were also a number of derelict tanks along the Poelcapelle Road. Ivan photographed two of these tanks that were both lost in action around the village of Poelcapelle on 9 October 1917 during the Third Battle of Ypres. Jack Lilley's battalion was in action around here at the time.

In the war history of the 4th Tank Battalion (also known as D Battalion), the fate of these tanks was recorded:

Ivan is very casually standing next to the wreck of tank D32, named 'Dop Doctor'. It was a Mark IV Female tank under the command of Second Lieutenant G.V. Butler, 7th Section of 11th Company, D Battalion.

> On 7th October tanks moved to St Julien and were camouflaged with brick rubble camouflage nets. At midnight the 8th/9th October tanks moved off to their starting points at Ritour Cross Roads. The possible avenue of approach, the St Julien-Poelcapelle Road was rendered difficult by 30 hours continuous rain, and to leave it was to become instantly ditched. Tanks were therefore compelled to proceed in column on the road itself.
>
> At Poelcapelle Cross Roads the leading tank ditched badly and was subsequently hit. The second tank received a direct hit near Poelcapelle Cemetery and burnt out. The remaining tanks were all ditched hopelessly in endeavouring to pass.

The route was evidently in a terrible state, steeped in mud, which made the tanks sitting ducks for enemy shells. Ivan's photograph of Wieltje illustrates how waterlogged this sector could get (see p. 174). D32 must have ditched at the side of the road while attempting to pass the lead tank that had already ditched. Ivan's photograph shows that it was subsequently hit on the right rear horn, breaking the track. It was also hit on the left front horn, breaking that track too. The tank was thus rendered completely immovable. D24 suffered a direct hit opposite D32 and on 23 October 1917 was tipped clear by another tank since it was obstructing the

Ivan standing on the wreckage of the D24 'Deuce of Diamonds' of 5th Section, 11th Company, D Battalion, which was under the command of Lieutenant R.G. Grant. The tank is also a Mark IV Female and the D32 can be seen through the wreckage.

road. Both tanks remained in situ until the post-war battlefield clearances in the 1920s.

Potijze, Zonnebeke and Passchendaele

The road that passes through the Menin Gate leads straight to Zonnebeke via Potijze and Frezenberg. At Potijze there are three cemeteries that Ivan visited in the grounds of the château: the Potijze Burial Ground, Potijze Château Wood Cemetery and Potijze Château Grounds Cemetery. This cluster of cemeteries was due to an advanced dressing station being located in the château grounds. This area was not far behind the front-line trenches and was frequently prone to shellfire. The château itself was totally destroyed.

Potijze Château Military Cemetery and the ruins of the château.

A dugout in the wood at Potijze Château, surrounded by splintered trees.

Further along the road is Aeroplane Cemetery, so named due to a plane that crashed in the cemetery. You then pass through Frezenberg before reaching Zonnebeke.

The remains of Zonnebeke Village.

Just past Zonnebeke is a road that heads north to Passchendaele, passing by Tyne Cot Cemetery. Heading east leads to Morslede.

The village of Passchendaele was obliterated during the latter stages of the offensive of the same name.

Ivan at Morslede, near Passchendaele, with ruins along the route.

Zillebeke

The commune of Zillebeke lies on the south side of the Menin Road near Hooge and includes famous battle zones such as Hill 60 and Sanctuary Wood. It is easily accessed from Hellfire Corner or from the Lille Gate. Hill 60, which had been formed out of the spoil from the nearby railway cutting, was of great strategic importance as it afforded advantageous views across the Ypres Salient. Therefore it became the host of bitter conflict and huge losses as both sides sought to maintain their grip on it. Thousands of men remain missing around here and the site has been preserved by the CWGC. Today you can still see the shell and mine craters and the remains of concrete bunkers (see pp. 68–9, 72–3 for photographs of mine craters).

Ivan frequently moved around this sector to visit several cemeteries, in particular Railway Dugouts Burial Ground, Bedford House Cemetery, Spoilbank Cemetery, Larch Wood (Railway Cutting) Cemetery, Woods Cemetery, Perth Cemetery (China Wall), Sanctuary Wood Cemetery and Zillebeke Churchyard.

Looking towards Ypres from Hill 60, a landscape full of watery shell holes. Zillebeke Lake can be made out in the distance.

Zillebeke Lake.

Railway cutting at Hill 60. The hill was formed from the spoil of this cutting. This area is now covered in dense vegetation.

The rusted shell of a land mine lies amid the cratered terrain of Hill 60.

A German pill-box on Hill 60.

Woods Military Cemetery near Hill 60. The cemetery was so named as it was separated from the front line by woods. The graves appear scattered and the ground overgrown, the woods destroyed, with the battlefields in the distance.

Zillebeke Church was reduced to a heap of rubble.

The Churchyard Cemetery of Zillebeke Church contains the graves of many officers and is also referred to as the 'Aristocrats' Cemetery'. Two of the grave markers were erected by their families prior to the introduction of the standard IWGC headstones. The war grave shown overleaf is for Lieutenant John H.G. Lee Steere of the Grenadier Guards and states that 'He fell in action near Zillebeke, 17 Nov 1914, aged 19 years.' He was killed by a German sniper.

Zillebeke Church and Commonwealth war graves in the churchyard in 2015.

All manner of debris, including pieces of duckboard and large shell cases, viewed from Observation Road, Zillebeke.

Two isolated graves can be seen to the right of this wrecked British plane in Sanctuary Wood. On 24 January 1919 Ivan noted: 'Take view in Sanctuary Wood with 7x5 [camera].' This is most likely the picture to which he refers.

About 1 kilometre east of Zillebeke is Sanctuary Wood. The wood was so named apparently due to the cover it provided to British soldiers from the front line in the early stages of the war. However, by November 1914 the name was far from appropriate. Aside from a military cemetery, today Sanctuary Wood hosts a museum and some of the best-preserved trenches on the Western Front.

When Ivan was exploring this area he found the wreckage of a British plane that had been shot down by the Germans. The pilot and observer were both killed. The white crosses to the right of the plane indicate where they were buried. They had to be buried at night as this place was under fire during the day and the bodies could not be removed. I have looked up British airmen buried in Sanctuary Wood Cemetery but cannot conclusively link any of them to the graves in Ivan's photograph (see page 193).

A preserved British trench at the Hill 62 Museum, Sanctuary Wood. I took this photo on a school trip in 1991.

The South Side of the Salient

The road that exits from Ypres through the Lille Gate heads south, passing by Bedford House Cemetery and then through St Eloi, Wytschaete, Messines and Ploegsteert, with Armentières just across the Franco-Belgian border. Kemmel lies just west of Wytschaete. It was along this section of the front that the series of enormous mines were detonated by allied troops on 7 June 1917.

The village of Wytschaete, known as 'White Sheet' to the Tommies, was severely damaged during the war due to its strategic value, offering good vantage points across the salient. Many mine craters from June 1917 are still clearly visible today in the vicinity such as that of Peckham Farm. It was caused by 87,000lb of ammonal at a depth of 240ft. A second 20,000lb mine ('Peckham 2') remains intact under a farmhouse shown in the immediate background of my photograph (below). It was abandoned after the tunnel flooded.

Peckham Farm mine crater looking east towards Wytschaete.

Ivan's motorbike on the Wytschaete hilltop.

Heading south from Wytschaete the road leads to Messines and then Ploegsteert. This town was known as 'Plug Street' to the Tommies, located at the southern tip of the Ypres Salient. It was considered one of the quieter sectors for British troops in Flanders until the German offensive in 1918. There are ten Commonwealth cemeteries in this sector; Ivan would often go to Ploegsteert to photograph graves at the London Rifle Brigade Cemetery.

Just to the east of Ploegsteert lay four mines in an area known as the 'Birdcage'. None of them were detonated on 7 June 1917, since the Germans had vacated the area by zero hour. One of the mines, 'Birdcage 3', made up of 26,000lb of ammonal, exploded during a thunderstorm on 5 July 1955. There were no eyewitnesses and the only casualty was a cow, but it left a crater 250ft across and 60ft deep which was later filled in. The other three mines remain underground.

Ruins in Ploegsteert.

A ruined house can be seen behind the London Rifle Brigade Cemetery in Ploegsteert. The two graves on the right are of Private O. Wheeler and Private A. Jones of the Worcestershire Regiment, both killed in action on 20 April 1917.

Berks Cemetery Extension which contains the Ploegsteert Memorial on which are inscribed more than 11,000 names of servicemen with no known grave. Just across the road is the Hyde Park Corner (Royal Berks) Cemetery.

Just 2 miles west of Wytschaete is the small town of Kemmel next to the Kemmelberg, a large hill that lies between Locre and Messines and provided the allies with good observation across the salient. The town suffered severe damage during the First Battle of Ypres in October 1914 but remained in allied hands until the Germans took the hill in April 1918 leaving the château, site of the main cemetery, in complete ruins.

A blanket of snow covers shell-damaged Kemmel, with the ruins of the church clearly visible in the distance. January 1919.

The ruins of Kemmel Church and the hill in the snow. January 1919.

A camp destroyed by shellfire, Kemmel.

View of the Kemmelberg from Lone Tree Cemetery, very close to the Spanbroekmolen mine crater which lies between Kemmel and Messines.

Behind the Ypres Salient

Ivan frequently visited or was billeted in so-called 'back areas' of the salient such as Poperinghe, Vlamertinghe, Reninghelst, Dickebusch and Locre. He also spent a fair amount of time at Bailleul, just across the Franco-Belgian border. These places would have had numerous camps, billets, army stores and supplies, artillery positions, field ambulances and medical facilities, as well as the military cemeteries. They were well behind the front lines for most of the war until the German surge forward in 1918 when places such as Kemmel and Bailleul were captured.

Poperinghe

The town of Poperinghe (now spelled Poperinge) lies just west of Ypres. Thousands of British troops would have passed through here to get to the front and many would have been billeted here. Ivan frequently visited Poperinghe and was stationed here at different times. The town has two military cemeteries and is very close to the more extensive cemetery at Lijssenthoek.

Photographic blend of Poperinghe Square looking towards the Town Hall.

Talbot House, famed for its hospitality and respite from the war, was established here by army chaplains Neville Talbot and Phillip 'Tubby' Clayton in December 1915. The house is named after Gilbert Talbot, brother of Neville, who was killed at Hooge earlier that year. Nicknamed 'Toc H', it was known as 'Everyman's Club' as all soldiers were welcomed in and told to leave their rank outside. Tubby Clayton's desire was to provide a place to rest one's soul and keep out of trouble; Poperinghe's night life tended to lure many a soldier into its dens of ill repute. Ivan used to go there to attend services in the chapel, known as the 'Upper Room', and play chess. He was there on the last night of the war.

Talbot House has been preserved as a museum open to the public and even offers bed and breakfast facilities.

The Upper Room at Talbot House. The wooden cross framed on the wall to the left of the altar is the original grave marker of Gilbert Talbot.

Some friendly advice from Tubby Clayton.

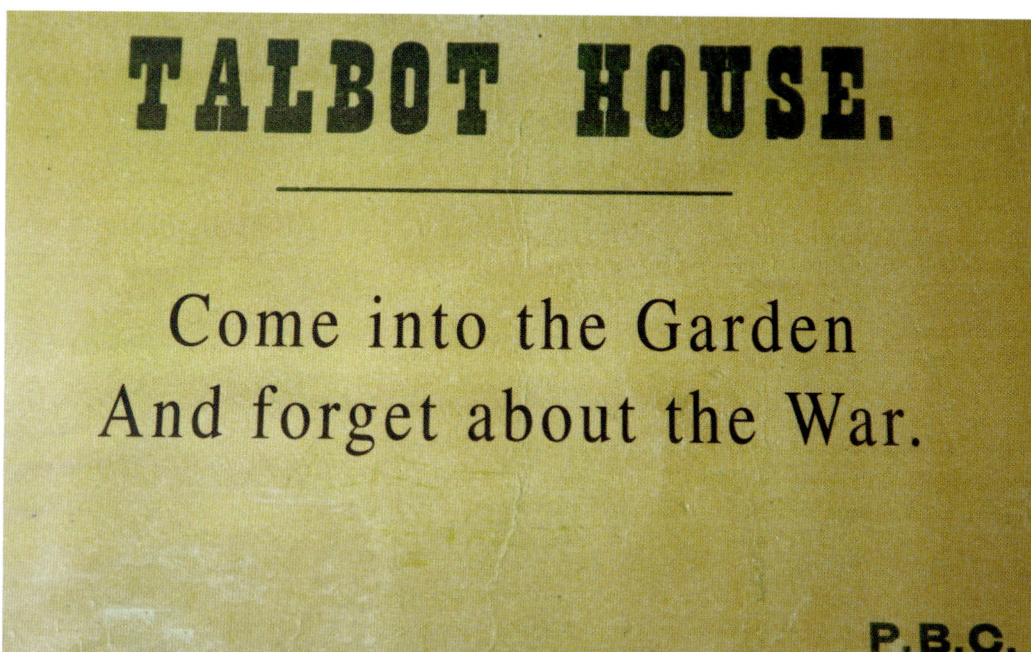

Corpus Christi procession passing by the shell-damaged A La Maison de Ville Estaminet, in front of St Bertin's Church in the main square, June 1919. The estaminet was not rebuilt and a war memorial has since taken its place.

A military ceremony in the main square on a dull misty day in January 1919.

Horses pull a gun through the square.

Ivan in Poperinghe.

Locre

Locre (today spelled Loker) lies in the south-western tip of Belgium close to the French border and was held by the allies for most of the war. Heavy fighting occurred here during the German advance of 1918 in which the village changed hands on several occasions. Field ambulances were stationed here in the convent which was used as a hospice. The hospice was completely destroyed by shellfire. Locre Hospice Cemetery features the grave of Major Willie Redmond who was MP for Wexford and a strong advocate for Irish home rule. He died of wounds inflicted during the Battle of Messines on 7 June 1917 and his grave was photographed by Ivan.

Ruins of the Locre Hospice, with the Kemmelberg in the distance.

Major Redmond's grave in Locre Hospice Cemetery.

The largely obliterated church at Locre.

The road from Bailleul entering Locre. A bus carrying troops can be made out in the centre of the photograph.

Bailleul

This French town lies close to the Belgian border about 8 miles south of Poperinghe. It was an important railhead, air depot and hospital centre. Many soldiers were camped or billeted here too, including Ivan and Jack Lilley in 1917. It was a Corps headquarters until July 1917 when it started to receive increased enemy attention and was severely pummelled during the German assault in April 1918.

Driver Griffiths stood by the motorcycle outside a destroyed billet on the Rue de Lille.

An estaminet is among the severely damaged buildings along the Rue de Lille.

Ivan on the motorcycle amid the ruins of Meteren about 2 miles west of Bailleul. This village took a severe battering from German guns in April 1918.

On 26 March 1919 Ivan wrote a letter to Viola about one of his motorcycle excursions from Poperinghe into France, arcing around the border and then back into the Ypres Salient along the Menin Road:

> On Monday I first took one of our drivers to the workshops at Cassel and then went off to Lille via Bailleul and Armentières. The road is good – pavée nearly all the way but there are some nasty little holes caused by shellfire which you come across unexpectedly. I went over one of these near Armentières and broke part of the front spring. I got some wire and fixed it up as best I could. Then I started off again going about 5 miles per hour. Just outside Armentières the other spring gave out on account of the extra strain and the poor old bike laid down like a tired doggie in the road (see sketch).

> I simply got off the bike and laughed at it. It looked so funny. There I was stranded – but not for long. I got some very strong wire and bound the thing together and set off for Lille going at 3 miles an hour. It took a long time but I got there eventually and reported at our D.A.D. office where I stopped the night. In the morning I took the bike to Loos (a small suburb of Lille) and went to a workshop for repairs. In the afternoon they fitted me up alright and I took one of the clerks in the side-car. He showed me round the town which was very nice. A small edition of Paris. I enclose a few more cards of the place. As it was too late to start back for Poperinghe, I stayed another night at the office and went to a good picture show. This morning I did a few things in connection with my photo work and took the clerk for another run in the direction of Roubaix. It was a jolly fine sunshiny day to start with but this afternoon it clouded over

and got very cold. I am afraid we are going to have a little snow. This afternoon I saw Major Fair, who has only just returned. The place where I interviewed him was too public to speak about promotion, pay etc but I was able to find out several things I wanted to know. Then I mentioned the loss of my camera [On 22 March Ivan wrote in his diary 'MC to Vlamertinghe, Railway Dugouts. Take 50 photos. Leave camera and films by roadside. Search all afternoon for them.'] I expected a row and a blowing up but all he said was, 'What do you think is the value of the camera?' I said, 'about £5.' He said, 'Well, this will come in useful if they should make you pay for the camera' and he gave me a £5 note. He said he wanted to give me something for the work I had done for him with his camera. Jolly decent wasn't it. I will send the note to Mother in place of the usual because if I am charged with the loss of the camera it will be taken out of my army pay and not out of my private money.

Then I got the old bike going and started for home. I came home via Halluin and Menin. A very interesting run. I gradually ran in to the area of devastation. Halluin and Menin were only slightly damaged. I bought some nice cakes in Halluin, but when I got to Gueleue [Gelewe] on the Ypres road I found only ruins and further on the villages of Gueluvelt [*sic*] and Hooge have quite disappeared. The road was in a hopeless condition and I had to travel very slow.

Nothing has been heard of my camera yet. I'm afraid it has disappeared forever. I have received my 26 dozen cards and shall set about selling them as soon as I can.

I can't think of anything more to say just now so chereo.

Your affectionate brother Ivan.

The Somme, France

The catastrophic casualties of the Somme offensive in 1916 created an immense backlog of work for the DGR&E but conditions didn't allow for that work to be adequately pursued until the following year. Fabian Ware wrote the following in a report just before the IWGC was established in May 1917:

> Prior to the Somme Battles of last year it had not been possible to organise burials during heavy fighting in the satisfactory manner which has now been done. Consequently, the Graves Registration Officers are still at work marking and identifying isolated graves in the areas of these battles. There are not less than 20,000 of these scattered over this wide and deserted district.

Graves Registration Unit personnel at Somme Camp.

According to Ivan's writings he was stationed around the northern Pas-de-Calais, Nord and Ypres Salient regions throughout the war. However, his photographs show that he did get to explore the Somme. He must have taken the following photographs in April 1920 when he made a special photographic trip on behalf of the War Office.

Albert

The town of Albert was a key location in the Somme, lying about 3 miles behind allied front lines. Many British soldiers would have passed through here on their way to the front for the Somme offensive. Ivan's photograph shows that it was a frequent victim of large amounts of shelling.

The ruins of Albert. The town is so battered that there is a sign attached to one of the trees that says 'Horse transport only'.

Albert Communal Cemetery Extension.

La Boisselle

On 1 July 1916 numerous mines were detonated along the Somme front by British troops just before zero hour. They had tunnelled under enemy lines and inserted enormous quantities of high explosive to blow them sky-high. Ivan photographed the 'Y-Sap' crater at La Boisselle on the north-east side of Albert, blown from a charge of 40,000lb of ammonal. This particular crater has since been filled in but there is another one that was blown at the same time close by: the 'Lochnagar' crater, which has been preserved.

The mine craters are most noticeably different to those of the Ypres Salient in that they do not resemble large ponds. The soil of the Somme is of a chalky nature compared to the wet clays of Flanders.

The Y-Sap crater. An officer and another man can be seen at the bottom of the crater, highlighting its enormity.

The Lochnagar crater in 2014.

Delville Wood

Delville Wood near Longueval saw very fierce fighting and severe casualties, especially among the South African battalions that fought here. This resulted in a large cemetery lined by the tree stumps that remain from the destroyed wood shown in the photograph below. The cemetery was created after the armistice from burials brought in from the nearby battlefields. It has 5,523 burials and commemorations, of which 3,593 are unidentified.

Thiepval Memorial to the Missing

This monument was not photographed by Ivan as construction began in 1928, but I have included it since it is the most imposing monument on the Somme landscape, visible for miles around.

This colossal monument was designed by Sir Edwin Lutyens and was unveiled by the Prince of Wales on 1 August 1932. Upon its walls are inscribed the names of 72,195 British and South African soldiers who have no known grave. At the foot of the memorial is an Anglo-French cemetery containing 300 British and 300 French graves.

Noyelles-sur-Mer

A base depot for the Chinese Labour Corps (CLC) was located at a place called Noyelles-sur-Mer in the Baie de Somme. As many as 96,000 men had been recruited into the Corps, of which 2,000 would lose their lives during the war or shortly after. Ivan took a number of photos of the CLC preparing the gravestones for the Noyelles-sur-Mer Chinese Cemetery, which contains 841 burials.

Men from the CLC setting headstones in place.

Noyelles-sur-Mer Chinese Cemetery awaiting completion.

My photo of a headstone in Noyelles-sur-Mer and the headstone of a fallen comrade being engraved by a Chinese mason.

The Iron Harvest

Every year the earth of northern France and Flanders yields a great iron harvest of hundreds of tonnes of unexploded shells, shrapnel, shell cases and fragments, bullets and barbed wire. When wandering around the Ypres Salient, especially in places like Hooge and Hill 60, it is very easy to find shell fragments and shrapnel balls on the surface of the earth.

Farmers have to use armour-plating on the underside of their tractors and other machinery as they frequently unearth ordnance which they leave at the side of the road for the bomb disposal unit to take away.

Rusted shell cases litter an area of preserved trenches and craters at Hooge.

What appear to be large gas cylinders stand with an unexploded shell, huddled together in a field in the Ypres Salient. These were discovered by farmers and have been left for the bomb disposal unit. This photo was taken while on a school trip in 1991.

The end of a grenade, Hooge.

The top of a shell with the fuse still intact, Hooge. The item to the left appears to be the remains of a toffee-apple bomb.

A ball of shrapnel found while wandering in the vicinity of Hill 60, photographed upon a war grave.

Chapter Ten

Ypres: From Ruins to Restoration

The Belgian city of Ypres marked a grand protrusion in the front line at the northern end of the Western Front. This salient was a key strategic allied stronghold that was to be 'held at all costs' to prevent the Germans from advancing to Channel ports such as Calais. It was therefore continually under attack from German artillery and aerial bombing throughout the war.

Ivan's photo of the Cloth Hall in ruins, with Belgian refugees and Tommies, blended with my photo of the restored town replete with tourists.

For much of the war the Germans enjoyed the strategic advantage of holding the high ground around the salient. In 1917 the British launched an offensive to break the deadlock in this sector and drive the Germans from their elevated positions. However, hampered by terrible weather and endless mud, the Commonwealth forces managed to advance no more than 5 miles, culminating in the Canadians taking the Passchendaele Ridge after more than three months of heavy fighting. Casualties were huge, amounting to around 600,000 killed or wounded between both sides. These allied gains were then lost by the following spring. It was not until October 1918 that the allies managed to push the Germans into a steady retreat from the salient, recapturing places such as Passchendaele and Messines, and Ypres was no longer in range of their shells.

By the armistice of 1918 this medieval city had seen five major offensives and was totally devastated without a building left untouched. The fervent defence of the Ypres Salient had left more than 200,000 British and Commonwealth soldiers dead.

Ivan first set eyes on the ruins of Ypres from the vantage point of Locre Hill on 5 June 1915, immediately noting the ruins of the Cloth Hall. The devastation was already apparent in the aftermath of the First Battle of Ypres in 1914 and was vividly described by an army chaplain, Reverend Edward Yeld Bate, in a letter to his mother dated 17 February 1915:

> The whole town is one awful scene of ruin and desolation, you cannot imagine a more pitiable, sorrowful sight. The fine old Cathedral and magnificent Town Hall one mass of ruins, the latter building contained a great deal of very valuable tapestry, pictures and art of every description. When the Germans shelled the town of course everything was destroyed. Scores and scores of houses in every street are entirely demolished, and every house bears silent witness to the terrible bombardments the place has been subjected to from time to time, every day even now they shell the town.

On 4 May 1915, during the Second Battle of Ypres, he wrote in another letter:

> The town was infinitely worse than it was two months ago when we were there. The old Cathedral, the Cloth Hall, and all the houses are now one mass of ruins, and the town is entirely deserted. I saw quite 50 horses lying by the roadside, and in the fields, some dying, others dead, they were in a dreadful state. Shells were still dropping in the town.

The ruins of the Cloth Hall, Ypres.

Since the Second Battle of Ypres up until just before the armistice the city had been a veritable ghost town, occupied only by troops billeted in the underground vaults of the strongest buildings, most notably the infantry barracks, the prison and the ramparts. By the end of the war it is said that a man on a horse could look right across the town, with barely a handful of buildings still standing.

Ivan was living in Ypres Prison when the German Spring Offensive got under way, making things very lively and increasingly dangerous. Later that year he described Ypres as a 'nasty place' and the Menin Road, which leads south-east out of the town, as the place that saw the 'worst hell of the war'; indeed, the general consensus is that Ypres has come to symbolize the enormous sacrifice of the British army during the war.

Sir Philip Gibbs, an official British reporter during the war, wrote an article for the *Ypres Times* (published by the Ypres League, a society for veterans of the salient) in October 1921 that described Ypres thus:

> The Ypres Salient is especially the greatest battleground of the British race. All our divisions passed through the furnace there at one time or other. Not one of them escaped that ordeal, and by general consent it was the worst place of all.
>
> It was a weak line that curved round Ypres and its ramparts – but it was strong enough to save us all, and the ragged ruin of the Cloth Hall in Ypres is a pillar

of victory gained by an immense sum of death now gathered into the graveyards where those comrades lie.

The desire to memorialize the sacrifice made at Ypres was inevitably going to be very strong. Winston Churchill, who was chairman of the IWGC, said in January 1919: 'I should like to acquire the whole of the ruins of Ypres...a more sacred place for the British race does not exist in the world.'

This would prove to be an over-ambitious whim that never came to fruition as former inhabitants returned to reclaim their city and initiate reconstruction works before the IWGC had been able to make much headway in negotiations about memorials. The Belgian government had formed plans to completely rebuild Ypres, but was acutely aware of the need to satisfy British sensibilities regarding this 'sacred' place. It was therefore suggested that the ruins of the cathedral and Cloth Hall and surrounding houses be preserved as a memorial park with a special 'zone of silence' in the centre. The town mayor had the area cordoned off with an insubstantial wire fence patrolled by a guard.

A teenage sentry stands guard amid the ruins of the Cloth Hall to ward off souvenir-seekers. The notice next to him reads: 'This is Holy Ground. No stone of this fabric may be taken away. It is a heritage for all civilised peoples. Town Mayor, Ypres.'

This plan, however, would also not come to fruition as the recently-returned citizens of Ypres strongly opposed it; they wanted their town back. The IWGC would have to settle for a purpose-built memorial elsewhere.

Ivan was able to capture the extent of the devastation in numerous photographs he took around Ypres once the restrictions on photography had been lifted, noted in his diary on 27 November 1918. In his memoirs he remembered: 'During my visit to our offices I saw that the army order forbidding the use of cameras had been cancelled so I immediately ordered a quantity of roll films and in my spare time took photos of interesting things in and around Ypres.'

The iconic ruins of the Cloth Hall and St Martin's Cathedral are a key feature of his photographs and are often visible in the distance. While recording the extensive devastation, his photographs also show how the city was attempting to return to some degree of normality as soon as it could, such as the rebuilding that began once former inhabitants were able to return. His photographs show all sorts of wooden buildings springing up like crocuses after a hard winter. These include an array of

This photo taken by Ivan near the ramparts was published in the *Daily Graphic* on 20 November 1919: 'War Shelters provide peace shelters. This quaint building at Ypres was made by a Belgian of corrugated iron from old dug-outs. He and his wife live at the further end, and the front part is an estaminet.' Many former dugouts and army huts around Ypres were transformed into such establishments.

cafés, restaurants, bars and hotels, there to cater for the numerous yet-to-be demobbed Tommies, the influx of construction workers, returning residents, battlefield tourists and pilgrims. A whiff of optimism is palpable in his photographs amid the ruins.

The Return of Refugees and Reconstruction

The war displaced millions of people along the Western Front. Once the struggle between British and German troops got under way in and around Ypres in 1914, thousands fled west to towns sufficiently behind the front line such as Poperinghe. Around 160,000 Belgians took refuge in Britain. As soon as the war was over, people started returning to see what was left of their homes and start rebuilding.

Returning refugees near Ypres Station, 1919.

Most buildings were severely damaged by four years of shelling and many were pulverized. It is evident from Ivan's pictures that many of the returning inhabitants had to rebuild their homes pretty much from scratch. By the spring of 1919 the Belgian government assisted many returning residents to find their feet, through the King Albert Fund, by building temporary prefabricated abodes on the Plaine d'Amour (the Minneplein today), the largest open space in Ypres. Demand for these wooden huts outweighed supply so subsidies were offered to others to build their own basic housing using whatever materials they could find from the ruins.

Men collecting bricks in preparation for building a new house, Ypres 1919.

'New Ypres' with fresh houses on the Plaine d'Amour in the north-west corner of Ypres. The Cloth Hall and cathedral are in the background.

The British had considered this space for a large international military cemetery, but it was rapidly overrun with emergency housing. Graves in this area would be limited to Ypres Reservoir Cemetery on the west side of the Plaine.

A new house under construction on the Plaine d'Amour, with ruins of the Cloth Hall in the distance.

A family poses outside their new home with a group of Scottish soldiers, drinking a health to New Ypres, near the Menin Gate in 1919.

Ivan's pictures also show several freshly-constructed hotels highlighting the increasing numbers of people that visited Ypres, desiring to make a pilgrimage to the cemeteries and battlefields. By 1920 the population of Ypres had reached 6,000.

A view from the ramparts at the Menin Gate in 1919. At least three hotels can be seen including The Splendid and the Hotel Ypriana. Horse-drawn bus carriages with 'Ypres-Mt Kemmel' written on the side can also be seen to the right.

President Wilson Visits Ypres

On 18 June 1919 Ivan was able to capture the visit of United States President Woodrow Wilson to Ypres. In these photographs the president is accompanied by King Albert of Belgium and the burgomaster of Ypres as they wander around the famous ruins. This visit was part of a wider tour made by the president while attending the Paris Peace Conference.

Mrs Wilson (with the dark sun umbrella) and Queen Elizabeth (with the white sun umbrella) are seen following behind President Wilson and King Albert.

Outside the cathedral.

Exploring the City

Using images captured by Ivan's lens and my own we can explore the ruins of Ypres compared with how it looks today. The Cloth Hall, St Martin's Cathedral and the Grand Place (the main square) provide an obvious central point of reference.

A map of Ypres town centre that belonged to Ivan.

The Cloth Hall and cathedral in ruins.

St Martin's Cathedral and the Cloth Hall in ruins. Standing on the vantage point from where Ivan took this photograph today would put you right outside St George's Memorial Church on Elverdingestraat. The foundation stone for the church was laid on 24 July 1927, one hour after Lord Plumer officially opened the Menin Gate. On the left-hand side of the picture the portico entrance to St Martin's Cathedral Cloisters can be seen.

The Cloth Hall originally took more than 100 years to construct, starting in 1200 and reaching completion in 1304. From medieval times it was the commercial heart of the city where cloth and wool were traded. It remains the grandest building, alongside St Martin's Cathedral, that the city has to offer. Its destruction by German shells and incendiary devices began in November 1914 and by 1916 a spoof advertisement in the satirical trench newspaper the *Wipers Times* described the Cloth Hall as the 'best ventilated hall in the town', 'ventilated throughout by Bosch and Co.' I need not describe how these buildings were by the end of the war; Ivan's photographs show this with stark clarity.

Reconstruction of the Cloth Hall began in 1928, under the direction of town architect Jules Coomans, with the belfry finished in 1934. It would take until 1967 to reach full completion, impeccably restored from the original plans. Coomans had a vision to restore all the prominent historic buildings of Ypres to their pre-1914 state.

The Cloth Hall and cathedral as viewed from the east side of the main square in 2013.

St Martin's Cathedral.

Construction of St Martin's Cathedral originally started in 1230 and was not completed until 1370. It was utterly destroyed during the war. Coomans started to rebuild it in 1922 using the original plans. It was completed with surprising speed by 1930 and was identical to the original building, aside from the tower having a taller spire.

St Martin's Cathedral in 2013.

Entrance to the cathedral cloisters. The sign leaning against it says 'Danger'.

Below: Artillery pieces outside a café called 'British Tavern' opposite the Cloth Hall. This was a temporary wooden building, painted sky blue, aimed at refreshing troops, builders and pilgrims alike. It was built by a Mr and Mrs Vercruysse on the site of their old business which had been reduced to rubble. Their daughter Germaine later married Captain Percy Parminter who had worked for the DGR&E in 1919. Today various cafés, bars, hotels and shops line this part of the Grand Place.

The Hospice Notre Dame at the east end of the Grand Place.

The Courthouse, a grand edifice built in Flemish Renaissance style, was built on the site of the ruined Hospice Notre Dame.

Within 200 metres of walking past the Courthouse you reach the Menin Gate. The 'gate' was more of a large gap in the ramparts through which passed the Menin Road, flanked by two seated stone lions. The lions were removed during the war to avoid their destruction. It was through here that countless British troops headed to the front line of the Ypres Salient, and thus was a very apt location for construction of a grand memorial. The site was therefore chosen in 1921 to build the Menin Gate Memorial to the Missing, designed by Sir Reginald Blomfield. It was unveiled on 24 July 1927. This proved to be the grandest venture that the IWGC could hope to agree with the Belgian authorities in respect of memorializing the river of British blood spilt upon the 'holy ground' of Ypres.

The ruins of the Cloth Hall and the Hospice Notre Dame as viewed from the Menin Gate in 1919. Walking along the left-hand rampart would take you south towards the Lille Gate. It was in one of the ramparts' casements along here that the men who produced the famous trench newspaper the *Wipers Times* were billeted.

One of Ivan's photographs of the Menin Gate in 1919 blended with my recent image, with the ruins of the Cloth Hall visible through the archway of the Memorial to the Missing. The memorial is inscribed with the names of 54,399 officers and men who have no known grave. The Last Post is sounded by the local fire brigade under the arches every night at 8pm.

Some of the names incised on countless panels of the Menin Gate.

Returning to the Grand Place and then walking slightly to the north of St Martin's Cathedral takes you to Rue d'Elverdinghe (Elverdinghestraat today). Heading westward this street leads to Ypres Prison where Ivan was based in March 1918. He had to set up his darkroom and sleeping arrangements in the cellar due to armour-piercing shells raining down on the building. As one of the sturdier buildings in Ypres it was considered a place of refuge, though repeatedly hit by German artillery. The prison was being used as a main dressing station when Ivan was there. During the Third Battle of Ypres it was used as a forward dressing station by the 9th Australian Field Ambulance. Ypres Reservoir Cemetery lies on the north side of the prison.

The entrance to the dressing station at Ypres Prison. There is a sign above the entrance which says 'Receiving Room for Wounded.'

A view of Ypres from the prison, with the cathedral and Cloth Hall clearly visible. Three Nissen hut dugouts can be seen just outside the prison.

The Water Tower near the reservoir, with the rear side of the prison in the background.

Photographic blend of the front side of Ypres Prison.

Continuing west, the Rue d'Elverdinghe leads out of the city centre across the railway line and onto the road towards Vlamertinghe and Poperinghe. At this point one would have found the ruins of the Ypres Asylum, otherwise known as the Hospice du Sacre Coeur. The building was used as an advanced dressing station, manned by RAMC field ambulances, and a British cemetery grew within its grounds, which Ivan visited on many occasions. The cemetery contained the graves of 283 Commonwealth servicemen which were all transferred to Bedford House Cemetery after the war. The asylum was badly shelled since it was situated along the main supply route to the salient. It was fully restored after the war and continues to be used as a psychiatric hospital.

'Ypres' is painted in large letters onto the ruins of the Ypres Asylum, heading towards the city.

Returning towards Ypres to the railway line, the station can be found within 300 metres to the south.

A panoramic view of Ypres Station, which appears to have been taken from Place de la Gare. The Kemmelberg can be seen in the distance.

This photograph, taken by Ivan, of the newly finished Hotel de la Gare, opposite the station, was published in the *Daily Mirror* on 10 January 1920 with the caption: 'Under the administration of King Albert's Fund, the restoration of Ypres is proceeding, and smart little four-roomed cottages and hotels are springing up among the ruins of this beautiful town. Above is a typical little hotel grafted to the ruins of a shattered building.' At the end of the road the Restaurant Skindles can be seen. I wonder whether Ivan took his panoramic shots of Ypres by climbing the very tall metal structure that reaches to the top of this image - though appearing precarious it is roughly in the right place.

I have stitched three images together to create this panoramic view looking over the railway line on the left side from Rue de la Gare (Stationsstraat), and overlooking Boulevard Malou (Maloulaan), facing north-westward. Zooming in on the far left side would show the ruins of the asylum and on the far right side the ruins of the prison. How Ivan achieved such elevation is unclear; presumably he was able to use an observation balloon or some fresh scaffolding.

A panoramic view of Ypres looking eastwards. The ruins of the cathedral and the Cloth Hall are clearly visible, as are the main square and the road heading east through the Menin Gate. This photo was taken from the same vantage point as the previous panorama.

This panorama, which overlaps with the preceding image, looks south-east showing the large infantry barracks on the right. Beyond the barracks you can make out the Post Office and the ruins of St Peter's Church on the Rue de Lille.

The front of the infantry barracks.

The infantry barracks were at the eastern end of the esplanade near the ramparts; an extensive complex, able to house thousands of men and used by the Belgian army before 1914. Many British officers and soldiers were based here during the war and no doubt made good use of the fortified shell-proof cellars. The walls were very thick and thus the safest billets in Ypres. It received its fair share of shelling but remained standing.

The interior of the infantry barracks showing rubble and damaged vaulting.

Following the ramparts along towards Ramparts Cemetery and the Lille Gate would have taken you to the cavalry barracks, situated one block west of the Rue de Lille.

The cavalry barracks.

A key road that ran south from opposite the Cloth Hall down to the Lille Gate and beyond was the Rue de Lille (now Rijselstraat). It featured the Hospice Belle, the Post Office, the Musée Merghelynck and St Peter's Church.

A view of Ypres taken from the ramparts. From the Cloth Hall to the left, panning across to the right shows the damage done to the Rue de Lille.

Ypres Post Office, the fourteenth-century Templars' House, was the least damaged building along the Rue de Lille and one of the very few buildings left standing in the whole of Ypres. Rebuilding began in the autumn of 1920 and was completed early in 1923.

An officer and two others stand by a Wolseley car at St Peter's Church on the Rue de Lille.

A similar view of St Peter's Church today.

St Peter's Church was built in the Romanesque style in the twelfth century and then rebuilt as a Gothic hall church at the end of the fifteenth century. Ivan's photos show that it was largely destroyed with only the vaults still standing. Coomans integrated the remains of the walls in the reconstructed church and chose to rebuild the tower in the Romanesque style.

Continuing south a little further along the Rue de Lille leads to the Lille Gate. Innumerable soldiers passed through here to the front line; a preferable route to the Menin Gate as it afforded much better cover from enemy artillery fire. Ivan passed through here to access cemeteries such as Bedford House, Railway Dugouts and the Voormezeele Enclosures.

Christ on the Cross survived the shells that destroyed St Peter's Church.

Ivan is in the sidecar outside the Lille Gate, on the south side of Ypres. His photo was taken in December 1918 or early 1919 and is blended with a current picture. On the right you can see a sign pointing to the Ramparts Cemetery.

The Lille Gate looking southwards, 1919. The sign above the doorway on the left side says 'A La Forteresse', a tobacco shop. Various British military units used this well-protected edifice throughout the war.

Leisure

In 1919 Ivan photographed various groups around Ypres, mostly GRU personnel and Labour Corps units. His photographic skills were clearly in demand and many a serviceman was willing to pay him for souvenir pictures.

Labour sergeants standing outside the cookhouse, Ypres.

Labour Company sergeants enjoying a drink outside their mess hut.

Two men from a Labour Company in Ypres, casually sitting among the ruins with an unexploded shell.

GRU football team. The ball has 'Ypres 1919' written on it.

Driver Greening, Joby and Ford car at Ypres.

Whit Monday – 9 June 1919 – was a day of 'glorious weather' ripe for private photography. Ivan took many photographs around Ypres that day as tourists thronged the city and the 48 Labour Company held a sports day.

Tourists gather outside the Cloth Hall.

Ivan wrote on the back of this photo: 'The orchestra at the sports held in Ypres consisted of a party of German prisoners and escort. The prisoners performed with violins made by themselves out of cigar boxes etc. They did very well.'

Tug-of-war at Whit Monday Sports, outside the infantry barracks.

The people of Ypres were keen to get on with life and determined to restore the town to its former glory; a feat that would evidently be achieved and would require much toil over subsequent years. Ivan's photographs clearly show the transition of Ypres from a place of death, destruction and hell to a place of life and leisure.

In 1925 the Ypres League published a guide called *The Immortal Salient: an historical record and complete guide for pilgrims to Ypres* in which it poetically describes how the city has undergone transformation:

> We picture the Ypres of war – ruin – desolation – emptiness. We step from the train to a brightly new and very complete town. We make our way through the streets to the central Place, and here a square of hotels, shops, houses stare across with strange incongruity to a mutilated thing rising stark and jagged against the sky. The ghostly witness, the symbol of all that has drawn us here, the ruined belfry tower rising from the ruins at its foot. This is Ypres today, a new venture, a newness of bricks and mortar clustered about this monument of a beautiful culture of the past, of unparalleled heroism in our day.

Wandering around Ypres today, if it were not for the numerous museums, cemeteries and memorials, you would never know there had been a Great War that tore the place apart.

Chapter Eleven

Back to Blighty and Beyond

By the summer of 1919 a number of Ivan's photographs give the impression that the intensity of his work had eased off somewhat, as his time in Flanders was winding down. He was able to visit a number of places that had previously been well behind the German lines since 1914, such as Ostend, Bruges, Ghent and Courtrai

Ivan (left) relaxing with Haddon and Cobb (who took the photo) at a café in Boulogne. By this point Ivan had been promoted to corporal and Haddon to staff sergeant.

(now Kortrijk). His 1919 diary shows that while he continued to visit numerous cemeteries, mostly around the Ypres Salient, he was increasingly able to dedicate time to private photography. He took many photos for his own interest, but also did a number of portraits and group pictures that he was able to sell. There was also more time for leisure activities such as rowing on the moat at Ypres and Brielen. The weather in 1919 was frequently inclement, compelling him to spend a large amount of time on clerical work, developing films and printing.

The following pictures show him and his GRU colleagues in a casual and relaxed light.

GRU personnel out on the moat at the Trois Tours Château where Ivan was based in Brielen from July 1919, on the north-west side of Ypres. The château became a base for battlefield tourism after the war. This photo of Ivan's features on the front of a brochure, produced around 1920, entitled *Tours through the Battlefields of the Western Front*, arranged by the Battlefields Bureau Ltd. It described itself as 'The finest centre in the Western Front, and within easy access of all points of interest by train, tram or car, and within easy reach of over 200 British Military Cemeteries.'

GRU personnel on a gun in Ostend. Ivan is furthest to the right.

Ivan, second from left, on the beach at Ostend, July 1919.

Graves Registration Unit personnel in Hotel du Cygne, Ostend, July 1919. Ivan is sitting on the right-hand side of the table, closest to the camera.

The invitation to a farewell dinner that Ivan attended at the Hotel Flamant. Judging from his diaries this was likely in Hesdin in April 1919. The other side bears the signatures of Ivan and fourteen other GRU personnel.

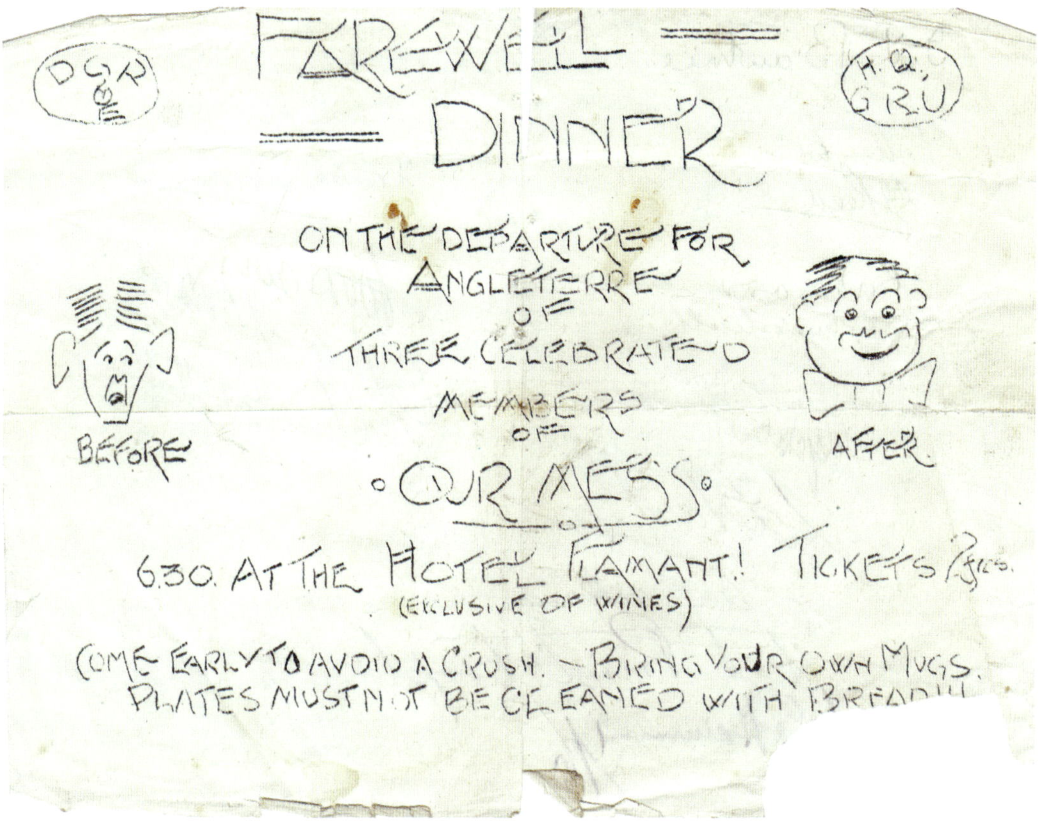

DGR&E

H.Q. GRU

FAREWELL DINNER

ON THE DEPARTURE FOR ANGLETERRE OF THREE CELEBRATED MEMBERS OF

BEFORE

AFTER

· OUR MESS ·

6.30. AT THE HOTEL FLAMANT! TICKETS [illegible]

(EXCLUSIVE OF WINES)

COME EARLY TO AVOID A CRUSH. – BRING YOUR OWN MUGS.

PLATES MUST NOT BE CLEANED WITH BREAD!!

I was kept in France rather longer than most because I had a great quantity of work to do, and only got my discharge in October 1919.

Arriving at London Bridge in the early hours of the morning we went by train to Brockley and marched all the way to Crystal Palace [used as an army demobilization station in 1919] where we went up the long glass covered entrance from Low Level Station [now known as Crystal Palace train station] getting rid of various equipment and getting papers signed etc until we reached the Palace itself.

There an officer stood on a chair, thanked us for our good service and we parted from the army. I arrived home tired but joyful in the early morning back to civvy life.

Demobilization came much later than desired for many servicemen after the war ended. Viola records in her diary that Ivan was due home on 29 September 1919 but was held up by the train strike. 'He's fed up with waiting to come home.' On 16 October she wrote: 'Ivan arrived home 11.30pm long after I'd gone to bed.' Athel had got his discharge on 22 May 1919.

Ivan was presented with this certificate of recognition from the British Red Cross Society in 1919. He was also awarded three military medals: the 1915 Star, the British War Medal and the Victory Medal.

President of the British Red Cross Society

Grand Prior of the Order of St. John of Jerusalem in England

BRITISH RED CROSS SOCIETY

Presented by the Joint Committee of the British Red Cross Society and the Order of St. John of Jerusalem in England to

Mr Ivan Lancelot Bawtree.

in recognition of valuable services rendered during the War.

Order of Saint John

Countersigned

Secretary

Chairman.

Vice Chairman.

1914 – 1919.

83, Pall Mall, London.

After demobilization Ivan was fortunate to be able to resume life much as it was before the war. He went straight back into his job at Kodak Ltd, working in the technical department, and was able to sell numerous prints from the Western Front to the press. On 11 November 1919 one of his photographs of Lijssenthoek Cemetery appeared in the *Daily Sketch*, captioned: 'The thoughts of thousands will turn to the little white crosses which mark the resting places of our brave dead.' Viola wrote on 12 December 1919: 'Ivan received £3 for his photos accepted by Press, and they want more photos.' Inevitably there would be much interest in Ivan's work in Flanders and Viola also noted that month: 'Ivan and Father didn't go to bed till 3 this morning finishing off Ivan's lecture. All went to it. Very good, except for poor light.'

However, it turned out that his photographic work on the Western Front was not yet over. In April 1920 Ivan was selected by the War Office to return to the battlefields of the Great War to take photographs of British cemeteries (old and new) to show the House of Commons what was being done. Viola commented in her diary that Ivan was selected 'because he's the best photographer.' He was assisted by the DGR&E and the IWGC to carry out this work and requested that they provide the following: advice as to the most suitable cemeteries to photograph and that he may be loaned a map to show their position; accommodation and rations where necessary; and petrol and oil for his motorcycle. Fabian Ware wrote a note endorsing Ivan to receive whatever assistance he required for this mission:

> It is hoped that all officers of the DGR&E and all connected with the IWGC will give every assistance to Mr Bawtree who has only been lent for a short time to the War Office and Commission to carry out this work. The provision of photographs illustrating all sides of the work, taken by someone who has real experience of it, is at the moment of the most importance but has to be completed in the shortest time possible. Fabian Ware, M.G.

Ware's message highlights the pressure that the Commission was under to complete the cemeteries as quickly as possible. He needed to show the government and indeed the public what was being done in a bid to lay to rest all the quarrelling that had interfered with the Commission's vision. Also by this time relatives were crossing the Channel in increasing numbers to seek out graves, which only elevated the pressure to get the cemeteries looking respectable amid all the devastation. The cemeteries were finally in the process of being transferred from the DGR&E to the care of IWGC gardeners and only the three 'experimental' cemeteries had been completed by this point.

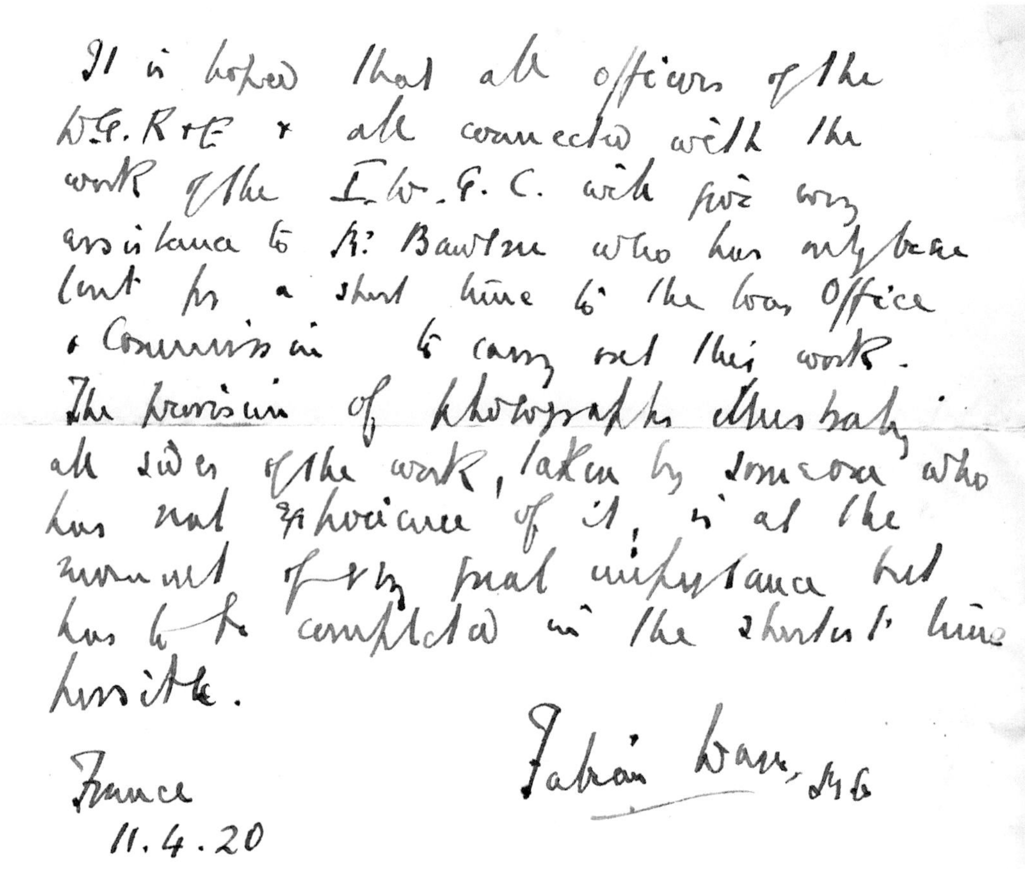

It is hoped that all officers of the D.G.R.&E. & all connected with the work of the I.W.G.C. will give every assistance to Mr Bawtree who has only been lent for a short time by the War Office & Commission to carry out this work. The provision of photographs illustrating all sides of the work, taken by someone who has not experience of it, is at the moment of very great importance but has to be completed in the shortest time possible.

France
11.4.20

Fabian Ware, MG

The original note from Fabian Ware.

An example of a completed cemetery at Louvencourt on the Somme.

Ivan sitting in the back of an IWGC Vauxhall car.

Ivan spent a whole month travelling to his familiar haunts of the front and in particular to the not-so-familiar areas of Arras and the Somme.

Ivan's mother Matilda pictured with a small dog-cart. She visited Ypres in 1920, presumably while Ivan was on his mission for the War Office.

After this assignment he could at last settle back into his work at Kodak. Aside from photography, his main interest was the Boys' Life Brigade. He went straight back to it after demobilization:

> I was then 25 years of age and was able to assist my brother [Athel] who had started a company of the Boys Life Brigade at Belmont Free Church. And that quickly became very popular. I think we soon rose to 45 members, and I was one of the officers. I had received my commission in 1914 actually. We undertook mostly first aid work, training in signalling, drill and my speciality was the trick card or transport which we had carried out in the Sutton Company which I had first belonged to.

He continued his leadership role in the Belmont Company, taking up the captaincy in 1926 when Athel stepped down to give more time to his photographic business. He also began another company in Epsom. At this point the BLB merged with the Boys' Brigade. Ivan was known to the boys as 'Cap' and Clapham Lodge became a hub for the BB as he would arrange many activities there. This included allowing those interested in photography to use a darkroom that had been put up outside the kitchen door. The large garden was ideal for annual fêtes – with races on the lawn – as well as a suitable space for laying out camping equipment before and after camps at Easter and summer, with tents laid out to dry and cooking pots and tent pegs everywhere.

The extent to which Ivan kept in contact with his friends from the GRUs is unknown. An 'Annual Reunion Dinner of the BRCS Mobile Unit and Graves Registration Commission' had been held since 1924. It is probable he attended many of these, but only the programme for the third one on 20 February 1926 survives, signed by those present, including Bert Haddon. Sadly Haddon died of cancer in 1927, having returned to the family-run pharmacy in Amersham where he worked as a chemist and optician.

The Second World War

During the Second World War, Ivan would once again experience the need to take refuge from German bombardments. Sutton was frequently visited by the Luftwaffe during the blitz of 1940–41, compelling him, his sisters, lodgers and any visitors at Clapham Lodge to descend into the cellar at the sound of the air-raid siren. Other relatives who were visiting, neighbours and members of the BB would also end up down there when circumstance dictated. It was clearly seen as a safe haven, and not just by those who lived at Clapham Lodge. Remarkably, the dates of all the raids can still be seen scrawled on the cellar's whitewashed wall.

One of the lodgers at Clapham Lodge throughout the war years was a German Jewish refugee called Julius Assenheim. Ivan recalled in his audio memoir:

> In 1939 Sylvia was asked if she was prepared to give hospitality to a Jewish girl [fleeing] from one of Hitler's concentration camps. Sylvia agreed but was flabbergasted to find that instead of a girl a tearful elderly gentleman, who didn't know a word of English, came to us. We took him in little knowing the wonderful help he was to be. He quickly learnt to speak English, he was able to do shopping, and took to gardening, although he had never done any of that before, and did marvellous work in the garden. In September I was evacuated with the firm [Kodak] to Harrow, leaving Sylvia, Elaine and Viola without a protector. But Julius Assenheim was wonderful in his ability and willingly cared for them all. He was very fond of Sylvia and they used to get on very well together. He didn't get on quite so well with Viola, although she put up with him. When the bombing came Julius was the man of the house and the family was cared for. In the bombing days we all slept in the cellar.

The threat of bombing after war broke out caused a large exodus from London. Ivan, in spite of being relocated to Harrow, still remained busy with the Boys' Brigade:

> I had to relinquish many BB duties, but I came home at the weekend and had the boys up to Clapham Lodge for training, and also I took the Bible class on Sunday. So I was still captain of the company, and while I was at Harrow I got involved in a company at Hatchend, and started one there at Hatchend Free Church. The war made no difference to our camping.
>
> Naturally many of our boys were involved in national service, either in the army, navy, or air force, or in civil defence, and were very successful in their services. We lost six members who were killed during the war, and we had a very creditable service in civil defence. During the war we ran a magazine called 'The Anchor' and seventy copies or more were sent to boys who were serving in the services. I was the editor. It was very worthwhile as we kept in touch with all the boys who were on service and gave news in this magazine of where they were serving and what they were doing and how they'd fared. I got away from Harrow in 1945 and was able to resume normal duties at Belmont.

Clapham Lodge remained unscathed during the blitz but the surrounding neighbourhood was hit on numerous occasions. Fortunately many bombs landed in fields or gardens and thus caused less damage than intended. Viola chronicled the blitz in great detail in her diaries. On 25 September 1940 she wrote about a very close shave:

> At 7.30 a woman warden came to the door, asking us to search our garden for time bombs. She said one had burrowed under a shelter in Southway (the road between us and Pine Walk) at 5.30 a.m. and it was that I had heard explode at 6.30 but all concerned had been evacuated straightaway. The shelter was demolished. She said lots of incendiary bombs had dropped and burned themselves out. Later we found one just behind the cottage. Sylvia found a burnt out one on the marrow bed by the cottage yard. It had demolished a marrow. She brought in the empty case as a souvenir. Several in the children's playing field. We learnt that a Molotov basket had burst and these were the results. Beans had one among their vegetables, next door to them had one, while the girls of the Riding School picked up 20 to 30 cases, and there were several in Furzedown Road. All had burnt themselves out doing no harm. A Molotov holds about 60. What a marvellous escape we've all had!

Then on 19 October 1940 she wrote: 'Sylvia went to see the big crater just off our road in a passage way to another road. Windows and tiles shattered but no other damage except to gardens, and no one injured.'

Moving to Harrow apparently wasn't far enough from central London to avoid the bombs. On 27 September 1940 Viola noted: 'Ivan arrived home early [from Kodak] because a land mine lay, unexploded, near their building.'

Having survived the Blitz, Clapham Lodge had a close call in late July 1944. Viola recorded that three 'flying bombs' (the V-1, known to the Allies as 'doodlebugs') landed in close proximity to the house and blew all the windows out. Many flower beds were covered in broken glass. The nearest of the bombs had landed about 200 metres away in a playing field. Fortunately no one was hurt and Viola commented: 'But that is small damage in comparison to what other houses and gardens are getting, and we can only feel very thankful. Our windows were all in need of cleaning, we had tried in vain for a long time to get window-cleaners so you can imagine how beautifully clear the outlook became when blast took all the neglected glass away!'

Photographs of blitz damage are conspicuous by their absence. One would have thought Ivan would have had plenty of opportunities to photograph the aftermath of air-raids, yet no such photographs have been found. Perhaps the novelty had worn off since the First World War. It is also possible that censorship at the time discouraged him from taking photographs since the government was keen to preclude the Germans from seeing anything that might appear demoralizing to the British.

The letter to Ivan from Sir Fabian Ware in 1941.

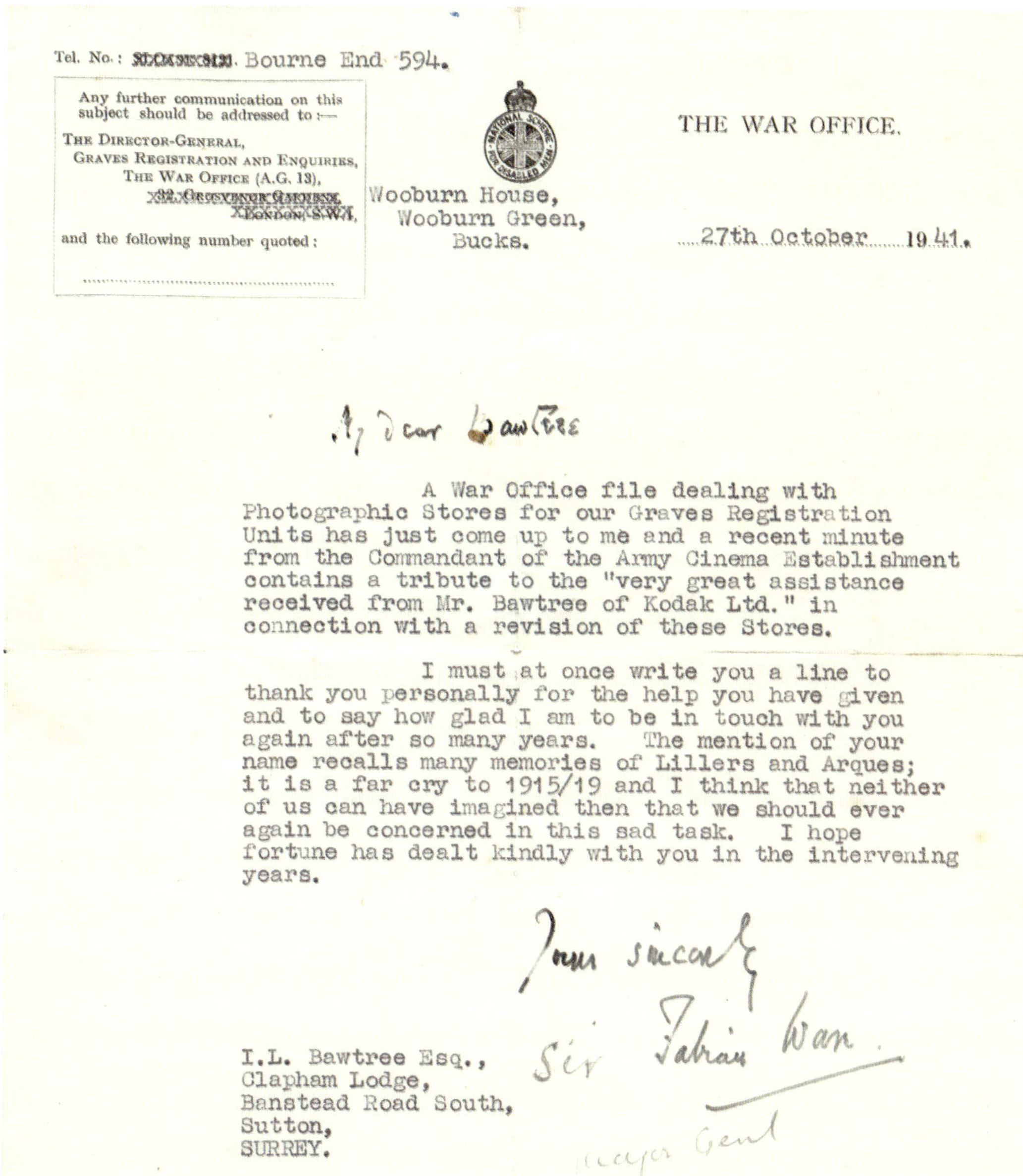

Tel. No.: Bourne End 594.

Any further communication on this subject should be addressed to:—
THE DIRECTOR-GENERAL,
GRAVES REGISTRATION AND ENQUIRIES,
THE WAR OFFICE (A.G. 13),

and the following number quoted:

THE WAR OFFICE,

Wooburn House,
Wooburn Green,
Bucks.

27th October 1941.

My dear Bawtree

A War Office file dealing with Photographic Stores for our Graves Registration Units has just come up to me and a recent minute from the Commandant of the Army Cinema Establishment contains a tribute to the "very great assistance received from Mr. Bawtree of Kodak Ltd." in connection with a revision of these Stores.

I must at once write you a line to thank you personally for the help you have given and to say how glad I am to be in touch with you again after so many years. The mention of your name recalls many memories of Lillers and Arques; it is a far cry to 1915/19 and I think that neither of us can have imagined then that we should ever again be concerned in this sad task. I hope fortune has dealt kindly with you in the intervening years.

Yours sincerely
Fabian Ware

Sir
Major Genl

I.L. Bawtree Esq.,
Clapham Lodge,
Banstead Road South,
Sutton,
SURREY.

In 1941 Ivan gave some assistance to the War Office in respect of its photographic stores pertaining to the Graves Registration Units. This prompted a personal letter of thanks from Sir Fabian Ware in October 1941. It is evident that Ware held Ivan in warm regard. Presumably these stores would have held the more than 28,000 images that Ivan took on roll film during the First World War. Unfortunately the stores were somehow lost during the second. While some records may have been lost when the Commission had to move its headquarters out of London to Wooburn Green in Buckinghamshire and others were destroyed as paper became scarce and the government called for recycling, the fate of the photographic stores remains a mystery. This is why the only photographs of his that survive are those that he kept in his cellar.

Retirement

After the Second World War, Ivan continued working at Kodak Ltd until his retirement just before his 60th birthday, having completed forty-one years of service. He was held in very high regard by his colleagues, both for his professional skills and his kindness. This is reflected by the album presented to him that contained everybody's signatures as well as transcripts of speeches from the farewell party on 30 December 1953.

Here are some excerpts from the speeches:

> Though he has been the longest in the Service Department and can be counted our oldest inhabitant in that sense, he is one of our youngest inhabitants in mind and spirit.
>
> It is just his spirit of helpfulness that has made him so many friends; especially so during the past five years when he had charge of the Sales-Service studio and darkroom here. How I must tell you that Mr Bawtree is a craftsman, and his place of work and his tools in the studio and darkroom have been used perforce by others. Some mornings a very livid but dignified gentleman has burst in upon me, swearing in the politest (but most blood-thirsty) terms dire vengeance on some representative or camera club member who has dis-arranged and (alas!) even damaged his equipment. After a while however he has invariably calmed down and become again his helpful charming self.
>
> All the while he has carried on his testing of roll and miniature film bringing to bear long and varied experience of practical photography to the Company's considerable benefit.
>
> Only a few months ago Mr Bawtree signified his wish to retire. We here today have made this opportunity to wish him well. Knowing him and something of his outside interests we know that he will be able to give more time to them. He has

his big house in Sutton to look after – Bawtree's Fortress, it is known as – and I understand he may even continue to do some photography.

Harold Carpenter, Chairman and Managing Director of Kodak Ltd, wrote:

> Certainly I don't remember anybody having such an array of gifts as I see here and when I look at this album containing so many signatures of his friends, I can say without being too sentimental that John [John is the English version of Ivan] has these things because he is loved by the people with whom he has worked. He has always been willing to give a helping hand to his colleagues, not only in the way of legitimate business, but in helping them out in the many photographic problems which come their way.
>
> This is a 'sinful' business and it is wonderful how John has been able to maintain his principles and integrity. Such men in business today are rare; his like are not often found. When the trumpets sound and we are all trying to get in at the Golden Gate, let us hope John will be there on the other side and, when we seek his help, let's hope he won't say 'No – you weren't in the Boys Brigade!'

Ivan sitting in the living room at Clapham Lodge with his retirement gifts on display: the collected works of John Buchan, the album of signatures and a pen and pencil set.

> Seriously, John Bawtree, I would like to thank you, not only for the work you have done for Kodak Limited, but also for the kindly way in which you have treated and worked with each one of us as individuals.

Ivan's MBE medal.

Upon retirement Ivan took up gardening, a pursuit in which he would have gained much experience in the fields of Flanders. By this point only he and Viola were still alive out of the six siblings. He kept going with the captaincy of the Boys' Brigade and in 1956 he was given a gold watch for fifty years of membership. He was passionately committed to the BB and its purpose that the boys who went through it would be 'influenced for good'. For Ivan the BB had provided him with a 'wonderful source of lifelong friendship'. He last camped in 1968 and was awarded the MBE in the New Year's Honours 1977 for his long service to the Boys' Brigade: 'At a climax to my brigade work and much to my astonishment, in 1977 Her Majesty the Queen honoured me by awarding me the MBE and I went to Buckingham Palace to receive this award from the hands of the Queen Mother. I received many letters of congratulations.'

When Viola died in 1973 death duties had to be paid, so all the grounds at Clapham Lodge were sold except for 30ft all round the house, and Ivan had a twenty-one-year lease. The house was photographed and listed. Ivan lived there until his death in August 1979, together with three lodgers. His life drew to a close as mine had just begun.

A photograph taken by my father: Ivan holding me in 1978, sitt with my mother at Clapham Lodge. The garden bench would e up at my family home.

Since Ivan never married, the clearance of the house in 1979 fell largely to the children and grandchildren of his brother Alfred, which included my father and grandmother. Apparently it was something of a 'free-for-all'. Consequently I grew up surrounded by numerous artefacts, such as framed Victorian photographs and 'Uncle Ivan's garden bench'.

Appendices

Numb. 30427. 13067

FIFTH SUPPLEMENT

TO

The London Gazette

Of TUESDAY, the 11th of DECEMBER, 1917.

Published by Authority.

The Gazette is registered at the General Post Office for transmission by Inland Post as a newspaper. The postage rate to places within the United Kingdom, for each copy, is one halfpenny for the first 6 ozs., and an additional halfpenny for each subsequent 6 ozs. or part thereof. For places abroad the rate is a halfpenny for every 2 ounces, except in the case of Canada, to which the Canadian Magazine Postage rate applies.

FRIDAY, 14 DECEMBER, 1917.

War Office,
14th December, 1917.

The following is a continuation of Sir Douglas Haig's Despatch* of 7th November, submitting names deserving special mention, published in a Supplement to the London Gazette of Tuesday, 11th December, 1917:—

ROYAL ARTILLERY.

Aikenhead, Lt. D. F., R.H.A.
Archdale, Lt.-Col. T. M., D.S.O., R.F.A.
Badham-Thornhill, Maj. (actg. Lt.-Col.) G., D.S.O., R.H. and R.F.A.
Barker, Lt. E.
Barry, Capt. F., R.H.A.
Bertie, Temp. Lt. (actg. Capt.) A. W., R.F.A.
Boylan, Lt. (actg. Capt.) E. T. A. G., R.H.A.
Browne, Lt. (actg. Capt.) V. F., R.H.A.
Codner, Temp. Capt. T. A.
Corbett, Temp. Maj. C. U., ret., pay, late R.A. (Maj., Yeo.).
Curling, Capt. (actg. Lt.-Col.) R. R.
Erskine, Maj. (actg. Lt.-Col.) A. E., D.S.O. R.F.A.
Flitch, Temp. Lt. J. E. C.
Gainsford, Maj. E. A., Res. of Off., R.A.
Gass, Lt. N. A.
Griffith, Temp. Lt.-Col. E. W.
Hamilton, 2nd Lt. P. W.
Harris, Maj. (temp. Lt.-Col.) O. M., D.S.O.
Hayley, Maj. W. B.
Hutchison, Maj. H. O., D.S.O., M.C.
Johnston, Temp. Lt.-Col. F. C. (late Capt., R.A.).
Kyngdon, Maj. (actg. Lt.-Col.) W. F. R.
Lister, Lt. A. R.
Lockhart, Temp. Lt. (temp. Capt.) N. C.
McMurtrie, 2nd Lt. (temp. Lt.) B. F., R.F.A.
Moultrie, Lt.-Col. H. C., R.G.A.
Murray, Maj (actg. Lt.-Col.) W. A., D.S.O.
Seagram, Lt.-Col. T. O., D.S.O., R.F.A.
Semple, Lt. R. E. W.
Skinner, Maj. (temp. Lt.-Col.) E. J., D.S.O., R.F.A.
Sykes, Maj. (temp. Lt.-Col.) F. B., D.S.O.
Thorp, Maj. A., D.S.O., R.G.A. (temp. Lt.-Col. R. H. & R.F.A.).
Ubsdell, Maj. T. R., Res. of Off.
Wainewright, Lt.-Col. A. R., R.H.A.
White, Temp. Capt. W.

* The list of names will be published in six separate supplements at intervals of a few days. 1. (11 December) R.N., Staff, Intell. Corps, R.F.C., Cav., Remount Serv., and Yeo. 2 (14 December) Artillery and Engineers. 3. (18 December) Infantry (up to S. Lan. R.) 4. (21 December) Infantry (remainder). 5. (24 December), Gen. List, A.S.C., Medical, Veterinary, Chaplain, Ordnance, Pay and Printing and Stationery Services, etc. 6. (28 December) Overseas Contingents.

13080 SUPPLEMENT TO THE LONDON GAZETTE, 14 DECEMBER, 1917.

Thomson, Temp. Lt. (actg. Maj.) A. C.
Thorne, Temp. 2nd Lt. J. E.
Trounce, Lt. H. D.
Tudsbery, Temp. Capt. (actg. Maj.) H. T.
Turner, Capt. (actg. Maj.) R. A., M.C.
Tyrrell, 2nd Lt. G. N. M.
Vanrenen, Lt.-Col. J. E.
Veal, Temp. 2nd Lt. T. H. P.
Vigers, Lt. (actg. Maj.) T. W., M.C.
Waghorn, Lt. R. D.
Wale, Lt. E. H.
Wallace, Temp. 2nd Lt. T. F.
Walton, Temp. 2nd Lt. W. E.
Warrington, Temp. Lt. (actg. Capt.) J. C.
Watkins-Pitchford, Lt. G. R. J.
Watson, Temp. 2nd Lt. B.
Weller, Temp. Lt. (actg. Capt.) F. G.
West, Capt. C.A., M.C.
Westwood, Lt. (actg. Capt.) H., M.C.
Whishaw, Lt. (actg. Capt.) W. B., M.C.
Whitaker, Lt. F. A.
Whitley, Temp. Capt. (actg. Maj.) H. S. B.
Wickham, Temp. Capt. (temp. Lt.-Col.) J. A.
Wilbraham, Maj. B. H., D.S.O.
Willis, Lt. (actg. Maj.) J. C., M.C.
Wilson, Lt. (actg. Capt.) W. G.
Wilson, Capt. (actg. Maj.) W. R., M.C.
Winterbotham, Bt. Lt.-Col. H. St. J.
Wooldridge, Temp. Lt. (actg. Capt.) A. E. S.
Worsfold, Lt. C. P.
Wrey, Temp. Lt. W. A. B.
Wyatt, Maj. (temp. Lt.-Col.) F. J. C.
Yorke-Eliot, Temp. Capt. (actg. Maj.) M. E.
Young, Lt. J. S.
Adlard, No. 107971 Corpl. (actg. Serjt.) G.
Aird, No. 49216 Corpl. J.
Alcorn, No. 94026 Serjt. D.
Anderson, No. 131518 Serjt. A. T.
Anderson, No. 12802 Serjt. (actg. Co. Qrmr.-Serjt.) E. W.
Angear, No. 62962 Serjt. J. L.
Appleyard, No. 248351 Corpl. J.
Archer, No. 41642 Serjt. C. E.
Armstrong, No. 144730 Lce.-Serjt. J.
Arthur, No. 106577 Serjt. A.
Ashcroft, No. 38570 Eng. Clerk Corpl. T. P.
Banks, No. 74025 Spr. R. H., Can. Corps., Sig. Coy.
Bannister, No. 22787 Spr. (actg. Serjt.) T. W.
Barlow, No. 100157 2nd Corpl. C. G.
Bates, No. 24914 Lce.-Corpl. (actg. 2nd Corpl.) J.
Bawtree, No. 130866 Spr. I. L.
Baxter, No. 49568 Serjt. E.
Bedford, No. 156417 Spr. A. J. R.
Beech, No. 207677 Serjt. W.
Beegan, No. 23275 Corpl. H.
Bell, 138128 Co. Serjt.-Maj. (temp. Supt. Clerk) A. J.
Bell, No. 118103 Lce.-Corpl. W. R.
Benham, No. 198246 Spr. (actg. Lce.-Corpl.) A.
Berry, No. 17964 Serjt. G. E. G.
Berry, No. 56298 Serjt. J. W.
Bilton, No. 88299 Serjt.-Maj. J.
Bilton, No. 41832 Corpl. W.
Bishop, No. 32824 Spr. (2nd Corpl.) C. A. N.
Blacklock, No. 20422 Spr. (actg. Lce.-Corpl.) J.
Boon, No. 146446 Corpl. J. R.
Borland, No. 253416 Corpl. A. F.
Boswell, No. 112196 Serjt. W. S.
Boucher, No. 50134 Lce.-Corpl. F.
Bowskill, No. 158085 Lce.-Corpl. S.
Bradbury, No. 95930 Lce.-Corpl. (actg. 2nd Corpl.) J.
Brooks, No. 97124 Lce.-Corpl. J.
Brown, No. 23107 Serjt. (actg. Co. Serjt.-Maj.) G. E.
Brown, No. 103267 Serjt. H.
Brown, No. 150578 Serjt. L. W.
Bruce, No. 107099 Lce.-Corpl. F.
Brudenel, No. 207703 2nd Corpl. F. E.
Burch, No. 62345 Lce.-Corpl. D. W.
Burnett, No. 69913 Serjt. W.
Burton, No. 82201 Spr. H.
Burroughs, No. 250007 2nd Corpl. A. F. W.
Butler, No. 148443 Serjt. H.
Button, No. 134260 Corpl. W. J.
Byrne, No. 35784 Lce.-Corpl. (actg. 2nd Corpl.) W.
Calderbank, No. 225684 Corpl. J. (killed).
Callaghan, No. 63839 Corpl. H. B.
Capon, No. 32425 Lce.-Corpl. (actg. 2nd Corpl. R. G.
Carter, No. 130734 Corpl. H. E.
Catherell, No. 78294 2nd Corpl. H.
Charlton, No. 27019 2nd Corpl. (actg. Corpl.) D. J.
Chaytow, No. 113147 Serjt. J.
Child, No. 53239 Lce.-Corpl. (actg. Corpl.) A.
Chilvers, No. 175140 Spr. (actg. Serjt.) F. S.
Christopher, No. 55098 Serjt. J. W.
Clark, No. 27274 Spr. (actg. Serjt.) Z. C.
Clarke, No. 16180 Spr. P.
Clements, No. 84800 Corpl. (actg. Serjt.) H. E. P.
Collcott, No. 88035 Serjt. G.
Collie, No. 1644 Supt. Clerk A.
Collinson, No. 104402 Spr. F.
Condy, No. 246767 Spr. E. B.
Coombes, No. 58237 Spr. F. J.
Coope, No. 308007 Corpl. T.
Cooper, No. 56351 Serjt. A.
Court, No. 66489 Co. Serjt.-Maj. H. R.
Courtier, No. 58617 2nd Corpl. (actg. Corpl.) C. J.
Cox, No. 176688 Corpl. F. V.
Cox, No. 12049 Serjt. (actg. Co. Serjt.-Maj.) H.
Craig, No. 23441 Serjt. (actg. Co. Serjt.-Maj.) F. G.
Crane, No. 18554 2nd Corpl. (actg. Serjt.) G. A.
Crisp, No. 52636 Corpl. G.
Crockett, No. 14880 Serjt. (actg. Staff Serjt.-Maj.) B.
Cullen, No. 45988 2nd Corpl. (actg. Serjt.) J.
Dagger, No. 43386 Dvr. T.
Dart, No. 56326 Corpl. (actg. Serjt.) J. C.
Davey, No. 240411 Serjt. W.
Devonshire, No. 25022 Lce.-Corpl. (actg. Corpl.) E. G. C.
Dorrian, No. 29447 Serjt. (actg. Co. Serjt.-Maj.) E. H.
Dowsett, No. 100511 Lce.-Corpl. (actg. Corpl.) H. J.
Downs, No. 229900 Spr. (actg. Co. Serjt.-Maj.) A. B.
Dredge, No. 15608 Corpl. (actg. Serjt.) R.
Duncan, No. 572104 Lce.-Corpl. (actg. 2nd Corpl.) A.
Dyer, No. 19394 Spr. J.
Eaton, No. 520021 Corpl. G. H.
Edge, No. 43245 Eng. Clerk, 2nd Corpl. (actg. Engr. Clerk Serjt.) D.
Edwards, No. 546200 Engr. Clerk Corpl. (actg. Engr. Clerk Staff Serjt.) J. W.
Ellen, No. 520012 Corpl. T. F.
Evans, No. 99086 Co. Serjt.-Maj. W. H.

Ivan's listing in Sir Douglas Haig's dispatch published in the *London Gazette* in December 1917.

Chronology of Major Offensives involving British and Commonwealth Forces on the Western Front 1915–18

Battle of Neuve Chapelle: 10 to 13 March 1915
Second Battle of Ypres: 22 April to 25 May 1915
Battle of Loos: 25 September to 18 October 1915
Battle of the Somme: 1 July to 18 November 1916
Battle of Arras: 9 April to 16 June 1917
Battle of Messines: 7 to 14 June 1917
Third Battle of Ypres (Passchendaele Offensive): 31 July to 10 November 1917
German Spring Offensive (*Kaiserschlacht*): 21 March to 18 July 1918
Battle of Amiens (start of the 100 Days' Offensive): 8 to 12 August 1918

Chronology of Where Ivan was Based

Château de Relingue, Lillers from June 1915
Arques Château from December 1915
School in Hesdin from April 1916
Château de Valfosse, Hesdin from October 1916
Bailleul from 9 February 1917
Estaires from 2 May 1917
Bailleul from 27 July 1917
Poperinghe from 9 December 1917
Dugout near Dickebusch from 9 January 1918
Poperinghe from 13 February 1918
Ypres Prison from 23 March 1918
Lijssenthoek from 1 April 1918
St Jan ter Biezen from 21 April 1918
Esquelbecq from 30 April 1918
Herzeele from 31 August 1918
Poperinghe from 10 November 1918
Ypres from 8 April 1919
Trois Tours Château, Brielen from 6 July 1919 (in tents from 27 July 1919)

Cemeteries Visited by Ivan

The following is a non-exhaustive list of cemeteries which Ivan is known to have visited as recorded in his diaries or featured in the photographic collection held by the Imperial War Museum. Where a photograph exists the IWM 'Q' reference number is given. Note that some of the smaller cemeteries ceased to exist as burials were removed to larger cemeteries following the armistice. In some cases the name was changed.

Ypres Salient, Belgium

Abeele Aerodrome Military Cemetery
Aeroplane Cemetery
Artillery Wood Cemetery (Q100621)
Asylum Cemetery (burials were later removed to Bedford House Cemetery)
Bard Cottage Cemetery, Boesinghe
Bavaria House Cemetery
Bedford House Cemetery (Q100692)
Belgian Battery Corner Cemetery
Bethlehem Farm Cemetery, Messines
Birr Cross Roads Cemetery
Blauwepoort Farm Cemetery
Brandhoek Military Cemetery
Buffs Road Cemetery
Bus House Cemetery
Buttes New British Cemetery, Polygon Wood (Q100601, Q100602, Q100922, Q100927)
Cabin Hill Cemetery, near Messines
Canada Farm Cemetery
Cement House Cemetery
Chester Farm Cemetery
China Wall Cemetery (Perth Cemetery, Q100544)
Cottage Garden Cemetery (burials were later removed from here to White House Cemetery)
Derry House Cemetery (south of Ypres towards Messines)
Dickebusch New Military Cemetery
Dickebusch Old Military Cemetery
Divisional Cemetery
Dozinghem Military Cemetery
Dranoutre Churchyard
Dranoutre Military Cemetery
Duhallow ADS Cemetery
École de Bienfaisance Cemetery (burials were later removed to Bedford House Cemetery)
Elzenwalle Brasserie Cemetery
Essex Farm Cemetery, Boesinghe (Q100418)
Ferme Olivier Cemetery
Frenchman's Farm (burials were later removed to Wulverghem-Lindenhoek Road Military Cemetery, near Messines)
Glimpse Cottage Cemetery, Boesinghe
Godezonne Farm Cemetery
Gordon Cemetery, Kemmel
Green Hunter Cemetery, Vlamertinghe
Gunners' Farm Military Cemetery (aka Lancs Farm), Ploegsteert
Gwalia Cemetery
Hagle Dump Cemetery, Brandhoek (Q100761, Q100805)
Halfway House Cemetery

Haringhe (Bandaghem) Cemetery
Hedge Row (Trench) Cemetery
Hengebaert Farm Cemetery, near Dickebusch (burials were later removed from here to White House Cemetery)
Hooge Crater Cemetery (Q100372, Q100373, Q100495, Q100928, Q100932, Q100933, Q100935)
Hop Store Cemetery, Vlamertinghe (Q100929)
Hospital Farm Cemetery
Hyde Park Corner (Royal Berks) Cemetery, Ploegsteert Wood (Q100740)
Irish Farm Cemetery
Irish House Cemetery
Kandahar Farm Cemetery
Kemmel Château Military Cemetery (Q100504, Q100696, Q100738, Q100739)
Kleine Vierstraat Cemetery, Kemmel
L'Ebbe Farm Cemetery, Poperinghe (burials were later removed to Perth Cemetery China Wall)
La Brique Military Cemetery
La Clytte Military Cemetery
La Laiterie Military Cemetery, Kemmel (Q100703)
La Plus Douve Farm Cemetery
Lancashire Cottage Cemetery, Ploegsteert
Lijssenthoek Military Cemetery (Q100530, Q100531, Q100572, Q100573, Q100702, Q100812 to Q100822)
Lindenhoek Chalet Military Cemetery, W. Flanders
Locre Churchyard
Locre Hospice Cemetery (Q100371)
Locre No. 8 Cemetery
London Rifle Brigade Cemetery, Ploegsteert (Q100493, Q100567, Q100743)
Lone Tree Cemetery
Lumm Farm Cemetery, Wytschaete (burials were later removed to Messines Ridge British Cemetery)
Malakoff Farm Cemetery, Brielen (burials were later removed to Duhallow ADS Cemetery)
Maple Copse Cemetery, near Hooge (Q100917, Q100936)
Maple Leaf Cemetery, W. Flanders
Marengo Farm Cemetery, near Boesinghe
Mendinghem Military Cemetery (Q100592)
Menin Road South Military Cemetery (Q100376)
Motor Car Corner Cemetery, Ploegsteert
Neuve-Eglise Churchyard, south of Kemmel
Nine Elms British Cemetery, near Poperinghe
Oak Dump Cemetery
Oxford Road Cemetery
Packhorse Farm Shrine Cemetery
Passchendaele New Concentration Cemetery (Q100924, Q100925, Q100931, Q100934)
Ploegsteert Wood Military Cemetery
Pond Farm Cemetery, W. Flanders

Poperinghe New Military Cemetery (Q100775)
Poperinghe Old Military Cemetery (Q100736)
Potijze Burial Ground Cemetery
Potijze Château Lawn Cemetery
Railway Dugouts Burial Ground (Q100691, Q100693, Q100754)
Ramparts Cemetery (Q100666)
Ravine Wood Cemetery (aka Hedge Row Trench Cemetery)
RE Farm Cemetery, Kemmel
Reninghelst Churchyard (Q100678)
Reninghelst Churchyard Extension
Reninghelst New Military Cemetery
Rest-and-be-thankful Farm, Kemmel
Ridgewood Military Cemetery, near Dickebusch
Rifle House Cemetery, Ploegsteert Wood (Q100741)
Sanctuary Wood Cemetery, near Hooge
Seaforth Cemetery Cheddar Villa
Solferino Farm Cemetery
Spanbroekmolen British Cemetery
Spoilbank Cemetery
St Quentin's Cabaret Military Cemetery
Strand Military Cemetery, Ploegsteert Wood (Q100742)
Talana Farm Cemetery, Boesinghe
Tancrez Farm Cemetery, near Ploegsteert
The Huts Cemetery, Dickebusch
Torreken Farm Cemetery, Wytschaete
Tyne Cot Cemetery, Passchendaele (Q100921, Q100923, Q100926, Q10030)
Underhill Farm Cemetery, near Ploegsteert
Vlamertinghe Military Cemetery (Q100454, Q100698, Q100777 to Q100779, Q100791)
Vlamertinghe New Military Cemetery
Voormezeele Enclosures
Watou Churchyard (west of Poperinghe)
Westhof Farm Cemetery, Nieuwkerke
Westoutre British Cemetery
Westoutre Churchyard and Extension
White House Cemetery, St Jean-les-Ypres
Wieltje Farm Cemetery
Woods Cemetery, Zillebeke (Q100748, Q100749)
Wulverghem-Lindenhoek Road Military Cemetery (west of Messines)
Wytschaete Military Cemetery
Ypres Reservoir Cemetery (Prison Cemetery, Q100397, Q100792, Q100793)
Zillebeke Churchyard

North-West Belgium
Adinkerke Military Cemetery
Coxyde Military Cemetery

Nord and Pas-de-Calais, France

Aire Communal Cemetery
Arneke British Cemetery (Q100746, Q100747)
Bailleul Communal Cemetery and Extension (Q100718 to Q100722)
Bertenacre Military Cemetery
Bois-Grenier Communal Cemetery, near Armentières
Borre Churchyard, near Hazebrouck
Borre Military Cemetery
Boulogne Eastern Cemetery (Q100704, Q100737, Q100780 to Q100782)
Caestre Military Cemetery
Cambrin Churchyard (Q100730, Q100731)
Chapelle-d'Armentières New Military Cemetery
Chapelle-d'Armentières Old Military Cemetery
Cinq Rues British Cemetery, Hazebrouck
Cité Bon Jean Military Cemetery, Armentières (Q100727)
Croix-Blanche British Cemetery, Fleurbaix (later removed to Y Farm Military Cemetery)
Croix-du-Bac British Cemetery, Steenwerck
Cuinchy Communal Cemetery (Q100717)
Desplanque Farm Cemetery, La Chapelle-d'Armentières
Ebblinghem Military Cemetery, between St Omer and Hazebrouck
Ecoivres Military Cemetery, Mont St Eloi (Q100773, Q100774, Q100776)
Eecke Churchyard
Erquinghem-Lys Churchyard Extension, near Armentières
Esquelbecq Military Cemetery
Estaires Communal Cemetery (Q100701, Q100724, Q100725)
Étaples Military Cemetery
Ferme Buterne Military Cemetery, Houplines
Ferme-du-Biez Military Cemetery, La Chapelle-d'Armentières
Ferme Phillippeaux British Cemetery, Houplines
Givenchy (Windy Corner) Guards Cemetery (Q100714)
Godewaersvelde British Cemetery
Gorre Château Military Cemetery (Q100729)
Halluin Communal Cemetery
Hazebrouck Communal Cemetery
Houplines Old and New Cemetery
Houtkerque Churchyard
La Gorgue Communal Cemetery (Q100726)
La Kreule Military Cemetery, Hazebrouck
Laventie Military Cemetery
Le Bizet Cemetery, Armentières
Le Grand Hasard Military Cemetery, Morbecque
Le Peuplier Military Cemetery, Caestre
Le Portel Communal Cemetery, Boulogne
Lillers Communal Cemetery and Extension (Q100734)
Malo-les-Bains Communal Cemetery

Merville Communal Cemetery
Meteren Military Cemetery
Meteren Mont des Cats Communal Cemetery
Mont Noir Military Cemetery, St Jans-Cappel
Morbecque British Cemetery
Nieppe-Bois (Rue-du-Bois) British Cemetery, Vieux-Berquin
Nieppe Communal Cemetery
Noeuse-les-Mine Military Cemetery (Q100732, Q100733)
Outtersteene Communal Cemetery Extension, Bailleul
Pont d'Achelles Military Cemetery, Nieppe
Pont de Nieppe Communal Cemetery
Ration Farm Military Cemetery, La Chapelle-d'Armentières
Royal Berks Cemetery (burials were later moved to Vieille-Chapelle New Military Cemetery) (Q100716)
Rue-du-Bois Military Cemetery, Fleurbaix
Sailly-sur-la-Lys Churchyard
Souvenir Cemetery, St Omer (Q100735, Q100797)
St Pol British Cemetery
St Venant Communal Cemetery, near Béthune
Steenvorde Communal Cemetery
Steenwerck Communal Cemetery
Terdeghem Churchyard
Terlinghem (Terlincthun) British Cemetery, Boulogne (Q100783, Q100784)
Trois Arbres Cemetery, Steenwerck
Vermelles Military Cemetery (Q100706 to Q100713)
Vieille-Chapelle Military Cemetery (Q100728)
Vieux-Berquin Communal Cemetery
Wimereux Communal Cemetery (Q100705, Q100785 to Q100787)
Winnezeele Churchyard
Woburn Abbey Cemetery, Cuinchy (Q100715)
Wormhoudt Communal Cemetery
X Farm Cemetery, La Chapelle-d'Armentières
Y Farm Military Cemetery, Bois Grenier
Zudausques Churchyard, near St Omer
Zuydcoote Military Cemetery, near Dunkirk

Arras, France

Dainville British Cemetery (Q100755)
Duisans Cemetery (Q100798 to Q100800)
Faubourg d'Amiens Cemetery (Q100769, Q100789, Q100790)
Villers-Station Cemetery, Villers-au-Bois (Q100806, Q100807)

Somme, France

Albert Communal Cemetery Extension (Q100757)
Bapaume-Post Cemetery, Albert (Q100758)

Bazentin German Cemetery (Q100808)
Bouzincourt Cemetery (Q100809 to Q100811)
Bucquoy Road Cemetery, Ficheux (Q100762)
Carnoy Cemetery (Q100752, Q100753)
Dartmoor Cemetery, Albert-Peronne Road (Q100759, Q100760)
Delville Wood Cemetery (Q100624, Q100766 to Q100768)
Doullens Communal Cemetery Extension (Q100772)
Forceville Communal Cemetery and Extension (Q100604, Q100873, Q100874, Q100876, Q100895 to Q100898)
Gordon Dump Cemetery (Q100788)
Haute Bagneaux Cemetery, Gézaincourt (Q100770)
Heilly Station Cemetery (Q100763 to Q100765, Q100823 to Q100825)
Louvencourt Cemetery (Q100613, Q100892 to Q100894, Q100889 to Q100905)
Maroeuil Cemetery (Q100801, Q100804)
Noyelles-sur-Mer Chinese Cemetery (Q100611, Q100878)
Puchevillers Cemetery (Q100771)
Quarry Cemetery, Montauban (Q100750, Q100751)
St Amand British Cemetery (Q100528, Q100529, Q100536, Q100584)
Sucrerie Military Cemetery (Q100756)
Villers-Fauconne Cemetery
Warloy-Baillon Cemetery (Q100744, Q100745)
Windmill British Cemetery, Monchy-le-Preux (Q100597, Q100612, Q100625)

Others in Northern France
Le Tréport Military Cemetery (Q100886 to Q100891, Q100906 to Q100909)

Bibliography

Primary Sources

Anon., *Ypres and the Battles of Ypres* (Michelin, 1919)
Barton, Peter, *Battlefields of the First World War: The Unseen Panoramas of the Western Front* (Constable, 2008)
Brown, Malcolm, *1918 – Year of Victory* (Pan Macmillan, 1999)
Cooksey, Jon & Murland, Jerry, *Battle Lines: The Western Front By Car, By Bike and On Foot – Ypres: Nieuwpoort to Ploegsteert* (Pen & Sword, 2012)
Crane, David, *Empires of the Dead* (William Collins, 2014)
CWGC, *Recovery and Reburial in 1919* (short publication, 2009)
CWGC, *The Ypres Salient* (short publication)
Dendooven, Dominiek & Dewilde, Jan, *The Reconstruction of Ieper* (Openbaar Kunstbezit in Vlaanderen, 1999)
Evans, Martin Marix, *Ypres: In War and Peace* (Pitkin, 1992)
Gibb, Sir Phillip, *The Line that Curved Around Ypres* (The *Ypres Times*, October 1921)
Hodgkinson, P.E., 'Clearing the Dead', article in *Birmingham University's Centre for First World War Studies Journal*, Volume 3:1 (September 2007)
Hussey, Christopher, *The Life of Sir Edwin Lutyens* (Country Life Limited, 1950)
Longworth, Phillip, *The Unending Vigil* (Pen & Sword, 2010 (first published in 1967))
Pulteney, William and Brice, Beatrix, *The Immortal Salient: An Historical Record and Complete Guide for Pilgrims to Ypres* (The Ypres League, 1925)
Reed, Paul, *Walking the Salient* (Pen & Sword, 1999)
Steel, Nigel & Hart, Peter, *Passchendaele: The Sacrificial Ground* (Cassell, 2001)
Summers, Julie, *Remembered: The History of the Commonwealth War Graves Commission* (Merrell, 2007)
Van Emden, Richard, *The Quick and the Dead: Fallen Soldiers and Their Families in the Great War* (Bloomsbury, 2011)

Family Archives

Memoirs World War I, Ivan Bawtree, date unknown
Diary for May to September 1915, Ivan Bawtree
Diary for 1917, Ivan Bawtree
Diary for 1918, Ivan Bawtree
Diary for January to October 1919, Ivan Bawtree

Episodes in the Great War, Viola Bawtree, 1914–19
Letter from Athel Bawtree to Viola Bawtree, 23 May 1917
Letter from Athel Bawtree to Sylvia Bawtree, 12 December 1918
Letter from Athel Bawtree to unknown recipient, date unknown
Letter from Ivan Bawtree to mother, 10 June 1917
Letter from Ivan Bawtree to mother, 27 October 1918
Letter from Ivan Bawtree to Viola Bawtree, June 1915
Letter from Ivan Bawtree to Viola Bawtree, 4 July 1915
Letter from Ivan Bawtree to Viola Bawtree, 22 April 1918
Letter from Ivan Bawtree to Viola Bawtree, 28 May 1918
Letter from Ivan Bawtree to Viola Bawtree, 16 October 1918
Letter from Ivan Bawtree to Viola Bawtree, 12 December 1918
Letter from Ivan Bawtree to Viola Bawtree, 26 March 1919
Letter from Oswald Stapley to Ivan Bawtree, August 1918
Letter from Second Lieutenant A.E. Hardy to Milena Lilley, August 1918
Particulars of Special Visit to Battlefields for Ivan Bawtree, Directorate of Graves Registration and Enquiries, April 1920
Service Records of Ivan Bawtree, searchable on ancestry.com
Album presented to I.L. Bawtree by his colleagues at Kodak Ltd, December 1953
War Office letter from Sir Fabian Ware to Ivan Bawtree, 27 October 1941
Bawtree History Recordings, audio cassettes recorded by Ivan Bawtree, c.1978
Clapham Lodge and the Bawtree Family, short book compiled by Anne Knee, 1990

Imperial War Museum Archives, London

The Bawtree Collection, more than 600 photographs taken by Ivan Bawtree; IWM reference PC 1419. Copyright held by Jeremy Gordon-Smith
Private Papers of Ivan Bawtree; IWM documents 2496
My War Diary 1915–1919, memoirs from private papers of Reginald H. Bryan, c.1920s–1930s; IWM documents 13953

Commonwealth War Graves Commission Archives

Draft Scheme for founding a Section for dealing with enquiries for Graves and applications for Photographs, Lieutenant Charles T. Wilson, 21 May 1915; File 30/GRC 5
Letter from Fabian Ware to Lord Robert Cecil, 5 May 1915; File 26/GRC 1
Report of the work of the Graves Registration Commission, Fabian Ware, 21 August 1915; File 30/GRC 5
Letter of thanks from David Davies to Fabian Ware on behalf of Herbert Asquith, 16 October 1916; File 34/SDC 4/DGRE files
Letter from Fabian Ware to Lieutenant Colonel Messer regarding the need to increase the number of photographers, 28 March 1917

Report of the Photographic Work of the Directorate, Lieutenant Colonel G.H. Stobart, A.A.G., 28 June 1918; File 34/SDC 4/DGRE files

Instructions regarding battlefield exhumations by Captain G. Crawford, taken from 'Exhumations – Report of Committee of Enquiry'; 1919, File 46/DGRE

The National Archives, Kew

Files concerning Lieutenant Edmund Arthur Howe Lilley, the Bedfordshire Regiment, 1915–1921; Reference: WO 339/42235

War Diary of the 1st London Field Company (part of 509th Field Company), Royal Engineers, December 1914 to August 1919; Reference: WO 95/1600/1

War Diary of the 130th Field Company, Royal Engineers, September 1915 to September 1916; Reference: WO 95/2236/1

War Diary of the 112th Infantry Brigade, January 1918 to April 1919; Reference: WO 95/2536/3

4th Battalion Tank Corps, War History; Reference: WO 95/110/6

Library and Archives, Canada

War diaries – No. 2 Canadian CCS, 14 April 1918, War Diaries of the First World War

War diaries – 46th Canadian Infantry Battalion, April and May 1917, War Diaries of the First World War

War diaries – No. 1 Company Canadian War Graves Detachment, May 1919, War Diaries of the First World War

Service Records of Edgar Leonard Bawtree (912023), Soldiers of the First World War 1914–18, Item Number: 29607

Other Archives

The diary and letters of Reverend Chaplain Edward Yeld Bate, 1914–15

Online Sources

www.cwgc.org (Commonwealth War Graves Commission)

www.1914-1918.net (The Long Long Trail, The British Army in the Great War, 1914–1918)

www.ancestry.com

www.iwm.org.uk (Imperial War Museum)

www.redcross.org.uk/About-us/Who-we-are/History-and-origin/First-World-War (British Red Cross)

www.ww1battlefields.co.uk

www.greatwar.co.uk

Index